Quick and Easy
INSTANT POT DIET COOKBOOK

Quarto.com

© 2023 Quarto Publishing Group USA Inc.
Text © 2018 Nancy S. Hughes

First Published in 2023 by New Shoe Press,
an imprint of The Quarto Group,
100 Cummings Center, Suite 265-D, Beverly,
MA 01915, USA.
T (978) 282-9590 **F** (978) 283-2742

New Shoe Press titles are also available at discount for retail, wholesale, promotional, and bulk purchase. For details, contact the Special Sales Manager by email at specialsales@quarto.com or by mail at The Quarto Group, Attn: Special Sales Manager, 100 Cummings Center, Suite 265-D, Beverly, MA 01915, USA.

ISBN: 978-0-7603-8358-2
eISBN: 978-0-7603-8359-9

The content in this book was previously published in *Thinner in an Instant* (Harvard Common Press 2018) by Nancy S. Hughes.

Library of Congress Cataloging-in-Publication Data available

Photography: Kristin Teig
Illustration: Shutterstock

The information in this book is for educational purposes only. It is not intended to replace the advice of a physician or medical practitioner. Please see your health-care provider before beginning any new health program.

DEDICATION

To "the Greg."
My husband, my best friend . . . my favorite person ever!

You would walk in the door after your own "pressured" day to pressure cookers in the sink, pressure cookers cooking away—everywhere you look, every surface is covered—and you just roll up your sleeves and chip in for hours . . .whew.

Thanks for being there . . . always . . . always!

Quick and Easy
INSTANT POT
DIET COOKBOOK

Make
Weight Loss
Easy with
Delicious
Recipes in an
Instant

NANCY S. HUGHES

NEW SHOE PRESS

Contents

Introduction: Are Electric Pressure Cookers Really That Great?

Electric pressure cookers can keep you from using the excuse "but everything's frozen" or "I'm out of time" to cook at home. Learn to rely on your pressure cooker instead. For example, you can . . .

- Start a recipe using frozen vegetables
- Thaw AND cook frozen ground beef and turkey in a matter of minutes
- Cook frozen, solid-as-a-rock boneless skinless chicken breasts in minutes that are t-e-n-d-e-r and juicy without any stringy, chewy, tough results—seriously
- Cook a dish that normally takes hours in a hot oven, or on a back burner that has to be monitored, in a fraction of the time
- Cook dried beans without soaking and serve them in about 35 minutes . . . from dried to table
- Make quick "pressure cooker" croutons and hardboiled eggs to include in a fresh green salad for a meatless entrée (with the definite promise of easy-peel, zip off shells)
- "Bake" potatoes in a fraction of the time that actually have the same flavor as those baked in a HOT oven for more than an hour

Types of Recipes in This Book

The varied recipes here include some protein combinations—some with vegetables, some with pasta or rice, while others can be served over veggie spirals, sautéed veggies, or riced veggies as a base—as well as soups, stews, and desserts.

There's a wide range of recipe types—from Mexican, Italian, Asian to Middle Eastern, Southern, and All-American—that include traditional beef stew to the popular ancient grain bowls!

The recipes in this book are designed to serve four. I felt there was a definite need to go that direction with so many smaller households just starting out or downsizing a bit. I found that the majority of electric pressure cooker cookbooks on the market include recipes designed to serve more. There are some recipes in this book that serve more than four, but only those that can freeze successfully so you can have them for another meal down the road . . . and they are tagged to let you know that.

Simple Ingredients, Short Directions

The electric pressure cooker is designed to make cooking more convenient and quick to help retain the nutritional benefits of your food, which is great. But I went a step further and did not include long ingredient lists or complicated, laborious directions.

I've written the directions in a way that will make cooking with an Instant Pot or other electric pressure cooker less intimidating. I was overwhelmed at first (probably like most of you), so I promised myself I would keep that in mind when writing the directions. Keeping the recipes simple to follow and even simpler to prep!

Since I don't know what type of electric pressure cooker you own, I've created healthy, low-calorie recipes to work in any standard electric pressure cooker. So whether you have the basic model or the "latest and greatest," you can make these recipes with successful, delicious, and healthy results!

I'm not taking you into every button on the pressure cooker, because each brand is a little different. But they all have a Manual button and a Sauté/Browning button of one sort or another. Since I want to keep things s-i-m-p-l-e, that's ALL I'm using throughout this book for your cooking functions . . . the Manual button and the Sauté/Browning button ONLY (and the Cancel button to switch between the two cooking modes). Extra (very minimal) equipment needed:

- Trivet (generally comes with your pressure cooker)
- Collapsible steamer basket
- 4 custard cups (6-oz, or 170 g, each) for desserts
- 8-inch (20 cm) nonstick springform pan for desserts
- Food scale for accurate weights of ingredients
- Ruler for measuring ½-inch, ¾-inch, and 1-inch (1, 2, and 2.5 cm) cubes
- Aluminum foil for slings
- 1-quart (946 ml) resealable plastic bags for degreasing
- Paper towels for skinning chicken legs and thighs

Pointers for Fast and Healthy Cooking

- When purchasing bell peppers, choose the wider, fatter variety rather than the narrower ones. They're easier to fill and keep their balance better while cooking.

- Watching your carb intake? Pick up a package or two of frozen riced veggies or spiralized veggies . . . or thinly slice low-carb veggies, such as zucchini, yellow squash, or snow peas, and cook a couple of minutes in the microwave to use as a base instead of rice, pasta, or potatoes.

- When shopping for fresh ginger, there is no need to buy a large amount, if only a small amount is needed . . . just break off what you need. The general rule is a 1-inch (2.5 cm) piece of fresh ginger yields about 1 teaspoon of grated ginger.

- When buying chuck roast, always buy more than needed for the recipe. Even with lean cuts, there's still a bit of fat to discard.

- To get more bread "surface" when making a sandwich using Italian or French bread, hollow out the center. Halve the bread lengthwise; remove the center portion of the bread, leaving a ½-inch (1 cm) border. You can then fill it with tons of veggies and a bit of lean meat or cheese!

- Purchase and use frozen ingredients, such as pepper stir-fry, corn, carrots, and so on, to reduce prep time. These easy-to-measure ingredients help make healthier meals when energies are low.

Flavor Finds

- Add a twist to a dish by reversing the marinade: Marinate with citrus or vinegar and oil, for example, by pouring it over the protein or veggies after they're cooked rather than before . . . the flavors will be more pronounced and there will be added moisture as well.

- Toast any nuts needed in a recipe, before starting the recipe, by cooking them for 3 to 4 minutes in a dry skillet over medium-high heat and set aside. This brings out the nuttiness without adding more calories or fat.

- Add a small amount, about 1 teaspoon, of instant coffee granules to give a dish a deeper, richer, "beefier" flavor.

- Squeeze a lemon or lime wedge over a dish just before serving to bring out the fresh taste of the other ingredients, and the saltiness without adding more salt.

- After ingredients are cooked, remove them from the pot with a slotted spoon. Cancel and reset the cooker to Sauté/Browning. Bring the remaining liquid in the pot to a boil. Continue to boil until thickened slightly and deep flavors develop. Pour the liquid over the cooked items to enhance the flavors and provide moisture to the dish without adding more fat, calories, or sodium.

- When a "meatier" dish is desired in a meatless main, add sautéed mushrooms, in particular quartered mushrooms

- If you're cutting back on sugar when making your favorite desserts, reduce the overall amount by ¼ to ⅓ cup (50 to 67 g) and add an additional 1 teaspoon of vanilla.

You won't miss the sugar because it isn't too drastic of a change and the addition of vanilla enhances the overall sweetness of the sugar itself.

- Adding ½ teaspoon of grated orange or lemon zest or grated fresh ginger pulls the flavors up.

Nutrition Nudges

- Add more vitamin C to your dish simply by replacing a green bell pepper with a red bell pepper.

- Add more protein to your dish simply by replacing light sour cream with low-fat plain Greek yogurt.

- Brighten up your white rice using ground turmeric when cooking, which turns the rice a brilliant yellow color and makes the other ingredients pop!

- Multigrain pastas are lighter in texture and color than whole-wheat pastas, but still provide a hefty amount of fiber and protein. Read the labels and look for pastas that are yellow rather than cream or tan in color. Oftentimes, this means they're higher in protein and lighter in texture than whole wheat pastas.

- One clever way to sneak more nutrient-rich veggies into your dishes is by puréeing carrots or red bell peppers (or both) into spaghetti sauce and tomato-based soups. It enriches the overall color of the dish as well.

- Incorporate more fruits into your day by cooking fruits and topping with ONE cookie, crumbled, such as a vanilla wafer or gingersnap, for a quick-fix crumble.

CHAPTER 1

Sandwiches and Wraps

When you think of sandwiches, the first thing that probably comes to mind is two pieces of bread with something in between—pretty boring, right? It's time to add some variety and brighten up the boring! Use tender lettuce leaves as cups to hold those sandwich fillings, make the most out of crusty French bread by getting the crunch without the carbs, and make "knife-and-fork" tortillas so you can stack ingredients high, really high. See? There's more to a sandwich than two pieces of bread!

Spiced Orange Chicken Bibb Wraps

SERVES 4: ½ CUP (85 G) COOKED CHICKEN, 1 TABLESPOON (15 ML) SAUCE,
AND 1 CUP (85 G) COLESLAW PER SERVING

FOR CHICKEN

2 tablespoons (16 g) sesame seeds

1 cup (240 ml) water

2 frozen boneless skinless chicken breasts
(8 ounces, or 225 g each)

½ teaspoon smoked paprika

⅛ teaspoon salt

¼ teaspoon black pepper

FOR SAUCE

¼ cup (60 ml) fresh orange juice

2½ tablespoons (50 g) honey

1 tablespoon (15 ml) canola oil

2 teaspoon Sriracha or other
hot sauce

1½ teaspoons apple cider vinegar

⅛ teaspoon salt

¼ teaspoon grated orange zest

4 cups (340 g) coleslaw mix

½ cup (50 g) finely chopped scallions

12 large Bibb or Boston
lettuce leaves

NOTE

It's important to let the cooked chicken rest for 10 minutes before chopping . . .
it will go from tough to tender in just those few minutes . . . those very important
few minutes!

Continued

To make the chicken: on your pressure cooker, select Sauté/Browning + more to preheat the cooking pot. Once hot, add the sesame seeds. Cook for 3 minutes, stirring constantly. Transfer to a plate and set aside.

Place the water in the cooking pot. Add the chicken and sprinkle it with the paprika, salt, and pepper.

Lock the lid in place and close the seal valve. Press the Cancel button. Press the Manual button to set the cook time for 10 minutes. When the cook time ends, use a natural pressure release for 1 minute, then a quick pressure release.

When the valve drops, carefully remove the lid. Place the chicken on a cutting board and let rest for 10 minutes to cool. Chop the cooled chicken into bite-size pieces.

Meanwhile, make the sauce: In a small bowl, stir together the orange juice, honey, canola oil, Sriracha, vinegar, and salt.

Press the Cancel button. Discard the liquid in the pot. Select Sauté/Browning + more. Add the sauce to the pot. Bring to a boil. Cook for 1 minute, or until it reduces to ¼ cup (60 ml) of liquid, scraping up any browned bits from the bottom and sides of the pot. Pour the sauce back into the small bowl, stir in the orange zest, and let cool completely.

To serve, place equal amounts of the coleslaw, scallions, and chicken in each lettuce leaf. Spoon the sauce evenly over all and sprinkle with the toasted sesame seeds.

NUTRITION FACTS

PER SERVING (230 G)

CALORIES	250	
		% DAILY VALUE
TOTAL FAT	9G	12%
SATURATED FAT	1.5G	8%
TRANS FAT	0G	
CHOLESTEROL	60MG	20%
SODIUM	270MG	12%
TOTAL CARBOHYDRATE	18G	7%
DIETARY FIBER	2G	7%
TOTAL SUGARS	12G	
ADDED SUGARS	10G	20%
PROTEIN	24G	
VITAMIN D	0MCG	
CALCIUM	64MG	4%
IRON	2MG	10%
POTASSIUM	375MG	8%

Tender Pork on Corn Tortillas with Avocado Mash

SERVES 4: ½ CUP (84 G) COOKED PORK, 1 CUP (47 G) LETTUCE,
2 TABLESPOONS (29 G) AVOCADO MASH, AND 2 TORTILLAS PER SERVING

Nonstick cooking spray, for preparing the cooking pot

1-pound (454 g) boneless pork shoulder, trimmed of fat, cut into 1-inch (2.5 cm) cubes

1 teaspoon smoked paprika

1½ teaspoons ground cumin

1 teaspoon canola oil

2 poblano peppers, seeded, and cut into thin strips

1 cup (240 ml) water

1 avocado, halved and pitted

1 garlic clove, minced

½ teaspoon salt, divided

2 tablespoons (30 ml) fresh lemon juice

¼ teaspoon black pepper

8 corn tortillas, warmed

4 cups (192 g) shredded romaine lettuce

1 lemon, quartered

NOTE

Bite into an explosion of taste and texture. Warm corn tortillas topped with garlic and lime avocado, tender pork and peppers, and crisp romaine . . . perfection!

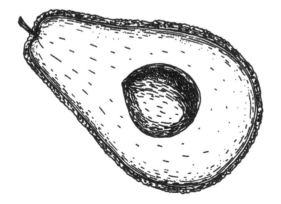

Continued

Season the pork with the paprika and cumin. On your pressure cooker, select Sauté/Browning + more to preheat the cooking pot. Once hot, coat the pot with cooking spray. Add the canola oil and tilt the pot to coat the bottom lightly. Add the seasoned pork in a single layer. Cook for 5 minutes without stirring. Stir in the poblanos and water, scraping up any browned bits from the bottom of the pot.

Lock the lid in place and close the seal valve. Press the Cancel button. Press the Manual button to set the cook time for 20 minutes. When the cook time ends, use a quick pressure release.

Meanwhile, in a bowl combine the avocado, garlic, and ¼ teaspoon of salt. Mash well. Stir in the lemon juice until well blended. Set aside.

When the valve drops, carefully remove the lid. With a slotted spoon, transfer the pork and peppers to a shallow pan or bowl. Sprinkle with the remaining ¼ teaspoon of salt and the pepper. Toss gently.

Top each warm tortilla with equal amounts of the avocado mixture, shredded romaine, and pork mixture. Squeeze lemon juice evenly over all and fold the ends over.

NUTRITION FACTS

PER SERVING (196 G)

CALORIES	320	
		% DAILY VALUE
TOTAL FAT	15G	19%
SATURATED FAT	3.5G	18%
TRANS FAT	0G	
CHOLESTEROL	70MG	23%
SODIUM	580MG	25%
TOTAL CARBOHYDRATE	21G	8%
DIETARY FIBER	4G	14%
TOTAL SUGARS	4G	
ADDED SUGARS	0G	
PROTEIN	25G	
VITAMIN D	1MCG	6%
CALCIUM	65MG	6%
IRON	3MG	15%
POTASSIUM	828MG	20%

Shredded Brisket Po'Boys

SERVES 6: ½ CUP (168 G) BEEF MIXTURE, 2 TABLESPOONS (30 ML) PAN JUICES, AND 2 OUNCES (55 G) BREAD PER SERVING

Nonstick cooking spray, for preparing the cooking pot

1½-pound (679 g) lean flat-cut beef brisket, trimmed of fat, patted dry with paper towels

1 cup (160 g) chopped onion

¾ cup (180 ml) dry red wine

¼ cup (60 ml) water

2 teaspoons balsamic vinegar

5 garlic cloves, peeled

1 tablespoon (6 g) sodium-free beef bouillon granules

2 teaspoons instant coffee granules

1½ teaspoons sugar

1 teaspoon dried thyme leaves

2 bay leaves

2 loaves (8 ounces, or 225 g, each) whole-grain Italian bread, halved lengthwise

¾ teaspoon salt

NOTE

When cutting back on calories, it can sometimes be difficult to include sandwiches made with French or Italian bread. Here's a way to get the bread you want and stay on track, too.

On your pressure cooker, select Sauté/Browning + more to preheat the cooking pot. Once hot, coat the pot with cooking spray. Add the beef. Cook for 3 minutes on one side. Turn the beef and top with the onion, red wine, water, vinegar, garlic, bouillon granules, coffee granules, sugar, thyme, and bay leaves.

Lock the lid in place and close the seal valve. Press the Cancel button. Press the Manual button to set the cook time for 1 hour, 15 minutes. When the cook time ends, use a natural pressure release.

When the valve drops, carefully remove the lid. Place the beef on a cutting board and let stand for 10 minutes before shredding.

Meanwhile, remove the center portion of the bread halves, leaving ½-inch (1 cm) border. The bread should weigh 12 ounces (340 g) after removing the center portion. Arrange the bread "shells" on a baking sheet and place them into a cold oven. Set the oven to 325°F (170°C)—there's no need to preheat—and bake for 8 minutes to crisp slightly. Remove from the oven and let cool. (The bread will become slightly firm once cool.)

Press the Cancel button. Select Sauté/Browning + more. Bring the liquid in the pot to a boil. Cook, uncovered, for 10 minutes, or until thickened slightly. Add the shredded beef and salt to the pot. Cook for 5 minutes to allow the flavors to blend. Spoon equal amounts on the bottom of each bread shell. Top with some pan juices and the remaining bread shell halves, pressing down gently.

NUTRITION FACTS

PER SERVING (184 G)

CALORIES	330	
		% DAILY VALUE
TOTAL FAT	8G	10%
SATURATED FAT	2G	10%
TRANS FAT	0G	
CHOLESTEROL	70MG	23%
SODIUM	580MG	25%
TOTAL CARBOHYDRATE	30G	11%
DIETARY FIBER	1G	4%
TOTAL SUGARS	6G	
ADDED SUGARS	1G	2%
PROTEIN	30G	
VITAMIN D	0MCG	
CALCIUM	57MG	4%
IRON	3MG	15%
POTASSIUM	269MG	6%

Lime'd Flank Tortillas with Guacamole

SERVES 4: 1 TORTILLA (36 G), 3 OUNCES (85 G) COOKED BEEF, ¼ CUP (56 G) GUACAMOLE, AND ¼ CUP (45 G) CHOPPED TOMATOES PER SERVING

⅔ cup (160 ml) water

3 limes

1 tablespoon (15 ml) Worcestershire sauce

2 teaspoons smoked paprika

1 teaspoon ground cumin

1 teaspoon Monterey steak grilling blend

1 pound (454 g) flank steak

4 high-fiber low-carb tortillas

1 container (8 ounces, or 225 g) prepared guacamole

1 cup (180 g) chopped tomatoes

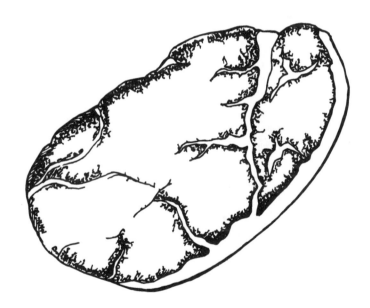

NOTE

The beef in this dish is cooked with lime juice, Worcestershire sauce, smoked paprika, and cumin. Then the liquid is cooked down to a rich thick paste and spread over the cooked beef, sliced, and served over tortillas with guac and tomatoes . . . words cannot describe how delicious it is!

In your pressure cooker cooking pot, combine the water, juice of 2 limes, and the Worcestershire sauce.

In a small bowl stir together the paprika, cumin, and grilling blend. Sprinkle the spices over both sides of the steak, pressing with your fingertips to adhere. Place the beef in the pot.

Lock the lid in place and close the seal valve. Press the Manual button to set the cook time for 12 minutes. When the cook time ends, use a quick pressure release.

When the valve drops, carefully remove the lid. Press the Cancel button. Select Sauté/Browning + more. Bring the mixture to a boil. Cook for 12 minutes, uncovered, or until the liquid is almost evaporated. (Note: It will appear to be a loose paste at this stage). Place the beef on a cutting board, spoon the paste over the beef, and let stand for 5 minutes before thinly slicing.

Warm the tortillas according to the package directions.

Cut the remaining lime into 4 wedges. Spoon equal amounts of guacamole down the center of each tortilla. Top with the beef and tomatoes. Squeeze lime juice over all, fold the edges over, and halved, if desired.

NUTRITION FACTS

PER SERVING (222 G)

CALORIES	320	
		% DAILY VALUE
TOTAL FAT	17G	22%
SATURATED FAT	4G	20%
TRANS FAT	0G	
CHOLESTEROL	70MG	23%
SODIUM	520MG	23%
TOTAL CARBOHYDRATE	13G	5%
DIETARY FIBER	1G	4%
TOTAL SUGARS	1G	
ADDED SUGARS	0G	
PROTEIN	31G	
VITAMIN D	0MCG	
CALCIUM	74MG	6%
IRON	3MG	15%
POTASSIUM	510MG	10%

Cheater's BBQ Chicken

SERVES 8: ABOUT ½ CUP (112 G) CHICKEN MIXTURE AND 1 BUN PER SERVING

2¼ pounds (1 kg) boneless skinless chicken thighs, trimmed of fat

1 cup (160 g) chopped onion

¾ cup (180 ml) water

2 tablespoons (30 ml) balsamic vinegar

2 teaspoons Worcestershire sauce

1 teaspoon smoked paprika

⅛ teaspoon cayenne pepper

⅔ cup (170 g) barbecue sauce, divided

⅛ teaspoon salt (optional)

8 whole-wheat hamburger buns

In your pressure cooker cooking pot, ombine the chicken, onion, water, vinegar, Worcestershire sauce, paprika, cayenne, and all but 2 tablespoons (32 g) of the barbecue sauce.

Lock the lid in place and close the seal valve. Press the Manual button to set the cook time for 15 minutes. When the cook time ends, use a quick pressure release.

When the valve drops, carefully remove the lid. Place the chicken on a cutting board, let it rest for 5 minutes and coarsely shred it. Place a colander over a bowl and strain the liquid from the pot, reserving ½ (120 ml) cup of cooking liquid and the strained onions.

Press the Cancel button. Select Sauté/Browning + more. Return the shredded chicken, the reserved cooking liquid, strained onions, and salt (if using) to the pot. Bring to a boil. Cook for 4 minutes, or until thickened, stirring occasionally.

Wearing oven mitts, remove the pot from the pressure cooker and place it on a heatproof surface. Stir in the remaining 2 tablespoons (32 g) of barbecue sauce. Serve with the buns.

NUTRITION FACTS

PER SERVING (155 G)

CALORIES	340	
	% DAILY VALUE	
TOTAL FAT	6G	8%
SATURATED FAT	1.5G	8%
TRANS FAT	0G	
CHOLESTEROL	100MG	33%
SODIUM	580MG	25%
TOTAL CARBOHYDRATE	36G	13%
DIETARY FIBER	0G	0%
TOTAL SUGARS	13G	
ADDED SUGARS	0G	
PROTEIN	26G	
VITAMIN D	0MCG	
CALCIUM	106MG	8%
IRON	3MG	15%
POTASSIUM	41MG	0%

So Sloppy Joes

SERVES 8: ½ CUP (125 G) BEEF MIXTURE AND 1 BUN PER SERVING

Nonstick cooking spray, for preparing the cooking pot

1 pound (454 g) lean ground beef

2 cups (270 g) frozen mixed vegetables

1 cup (150 g) chopped green bell pepper

½ cup (120 ml) water

1½ tablespoons (23 ml) Worcestershire sauce

1 tablespoon (15 ml) balsamic vinegar

2 teaspoons ground cumin

1 teaspoon smoked paprika

½ cup (130 g) tomato paste

2 teaspoons sugar

¾ teaspoon salt

8 whole-wheat hamburger buns, toasted

On your pressure cooker, select Sauté/Browning + more to preheat the cooking pot. Once hot, coat the pot with cooking spray. Add the ground beef. Cook for about 3 minutes until no longer pink, stirring occasionally. Add the frozen vegetables, green bell pepper, water, Worcestershire sauce, vinegar, cumin, and paprika. Spoon the tomato paste on top and sprinkle evenly with the sugar. Do not stir.

Lock the lid in place and close the seal valve. Press the Cancel button. Press the Manual button to set the cook time for 5 minutes. When the cook time ends, use a quick pressure release.

When the valve drops, carefully remove the lid. Stir in the salt. Serve over the hamburger buns.

NUTRITION FACTS

PER SERVING (174 G)

CALORIES	280	
	% DAILY VALUE	
TOTAL FAT	7G	9%
SATURATED FAT	2.5G	13%
TRANS FAT	0G	
CHOLESTEROL	35MG	12%
SODIUM	660MG	29%
TOTAL CARBOHYDRATE	36G	13%
DIETARY FIBER	0G	
TOTAL SUGARS	9G	
ADDED SUGARS	1G	2%
PROTEIN	20G	
VITAMIN D	0MCG	
CALCIUM	130MG	10%
IRON	2MG	10%
POTASSIUM	356MG	8%

Beef Hoagies

SERVES 8: ½ CUP (74 G) BEEF, ABOUT ¼ CUP (32 G) PEPPER MIXTURE,
2 TABLESPOONS (30 ML) DIPPING SAUCE, AND 1 ROLL PER SERVING

Nonstick cooking spray, for preparing the cooking pot

2 red bell peppers (or 1 red pepper and 1 yellow pepper), thinly sliced

⅓ cup (40 g) sliced pepperoncini

2-pound (908 g) lean boneless chuck roast, cut into 4 to 6 pieces, trimmed of fat

½ cup (120 ml) red wine

⅓ cup (80 ml) water

1 tablespoon (15 ml) Worcestershire sauce

2 teaspoons dried Italian seasoning

1 teaspoon garlic powder

¾ teaspoon salt

½ teaspoon black pepper

8 hoagie rolls (2 ounces, or 55g, each)

NOTE

You can purchase sliced pepperoncini peppers in the olive and pickle aisle of major supermarkets, but if you find only whole, just slice them into thin rounds. Don't substitute another pepper; they add personality and punch to the hoagies.

On your pressure cooker, select Sauté/Browning + more to preheat the cooking pot. Once hot, coat the pot with cooking spray. Add the bell peppers. Cook for 8 minutes, or until lightly browned on the edges, stirring occasionally. Stir in the pepperoncini. Cook for 15 seconds. Transfer the pepper mixture to a plate and set aside.

Coat the pot again with cooking spray. Add half the beef. Cook *without turning* for 5 minutes. Turn the beef and add the red wine, water, Worcestershire sauce, Italian seasoning, garlic powder, salt, and pepper.

Lock the lid in place and close the seal valve. Press the Cancel button. Press the Manual button to set the cook time for 40 minutes. When the cook time ends, use a natural pressure release.

When the valve drops, carefully remove the lid. Remove the beef from the pot and coarsely shred. Turn off the pressure cooker. Pour the pan juices into a fat separator. (Alternatively, place the liquid in a resealable freezer bag. Allow the fat to rise to the top. Hold the bag over a 2-cup [480 ml] measuring cup, snip one end of the bag, and allow the pan juices to flow into the measuring cup. Stop the flow when it comes close to the fat.) Discard the fat and return the pan juices to the pressure cooker pot.

Place equal amounts of beef on each roll. Top with the pepper mixture and serve with the dipping sauce.

NUTRITION FACTS

PER SERVING (176 G)

CALORIES	350	
		% DAILY VALUE
TOTAL FAT	12G	15%
SATURATED FAT	3.5G	18%
TRANS FAT	0G	
CHOLESTEROL	60MG	20%
SODIUM	630MG	27%
TOTAL CARBOHYDRATE	30G	11%
DIETARY FIBER	1G	4%
TOTAL SUGARS	4G	
ADDED SUGARS	0G	
PROTEIN	26G	
VITAMIN D	0MCG	
CALCIUM	82MG	6%
IRON	3MG	15%
POTASSIUM	242MG	6%

Lebanese Beef and Pecan–Stuffed Pitas

SERVES 4: ¾ CUP (212 G) BEEF MIXTURE, ½ PITA ROUND, AND
1 TABLESPOON (15 G) YOGURT

2 ounces (55 g) chopped pecans

1 cup (240 ml) water

1 cup (160 g) chopped onion

½ teaspoon ground cinnamon

½ teaspoon ground cumin

¼ teaspoon ground allspice

⅛ teaspoon red pepper flakes

1 pound (454 g) frozen extra-lean ground beef

1 tablespoon (15 g) ketchup

½ teaspoon salt

⅛ teaspoon black pepper

2 white or whole-wheat pita rounds (about
6 inches, or 15 cm),
halved and warmed

¼ cup (60 g) plain 2% Greek yogurt

On your pressure cooker cooking pot, select Sauté/Browning + more to preheat the cooking pot. Once hot, add the pecans to the pot. Cook for 4 minutes, stirring occasionally. Remove and set aside. Add the water to the cooking pot. Stir in the onion, cinnamon, cumin, allspice, and red pepper flakes. Add the frozen ground beef.

Lock the lid in place and close the seal valve. Press the Cancel button. Press the Manual button to set the cook time for 5 minutes. When the cook time ends, use a quick pressure release.

When the valve drops, carefully remove the lid. Press the Cancel button. Select Sauté/Browning + more. Stir in the ketchup, salt, black pepper, and pecans. Cook for 8 to 10 minutes, or until the liquid is almost evaporated, stirring to break up larger pieces of beef while cooking (some liquid should still remain).

Spoon equal amounts of the beef mixture into each pita half. Top each with 1 tablespoon (15 g) of yogurt.

NUTRITION FACTS

SERVING SIZE (212 G)		
CALORIES	320	
	% DAILY VALUE	
TOTAL FAT	14G	18%
SATURATED FAT	4.5G	23%
TRANS FAT	0G	
CHOLESTEROL	70MG	23%
SODIUM	580MG	25%
TOTAL CARBOHYDRATE	24G	9%
DIETARY FIBER	1G	4%
TOTAL SUGARS	4G	
ADDED SUGARS	1G	2%
PROTEIN	29G	
VITAMIN D	0MCG	
CALCIUM	34MG	2%
IRON	1MG	6%
POTASSIUM	154MG	4%

CHAPTER 2

Main-Course Salads

Salads…in a pressure cooker? Really? Why? Because you can broaden your salad choices and salad ingredients by being able to transform frozen, hard-as-a-rock chicken or salmon into tender, "salad-ready" ingredients in a fraction of the time. You can cook lentils and dried beans in a flash! You can even make hard cooked eggs with shells that literally slip off…no bits of shell stuck to the eggs…ever! Another thing you can do is double up the items you're pressure cooking to keep extra (chicken, fish, lentils or eggs) on hand for another use later in the week. That helps to simplify your meals, too! That's why the pressure cooker is such a great tool!

Curried Chicken Salad on Melon

SERVES 4: 1 CUP (96 G) CHICKEN SALAD PLUS 2 MELON WEDGES PER SERVING

1 ounce (28 g) slivered almonds

12 ounces (340 g) frozen boneless skinless chicken breasts

1 cup (240 ml) water

1½ teaspoons curry powder, divided

1 can (8 ounces, or 225 g) sliced water chestnuts, drained and chopped

½ cup (75 g) raisins, preferably golden

¼ cup (115 g) light mayonnaise

2 tablespoons (30 ml) fresh lemon juice

2 tablespoons (20 g) finely chopped red onion

¼ teaspoon ground cumin

¼ teaspoon salt

Pinch of cayenne pepper

1 small cantaloupe, peeled, seeded, and cut into 8 wedges

On your pressure cooker, select Sauté/Browning + more to preheat the cooking pot. Once hot, add the almonds. Cook for 4 minutes, stirring occasionally, until fragrant or just beginning to lightly brown. Transfer to a plate and set aside.

In the pot, combine the chicken and water. Sprinkle with ½ teaspoon of curry powder.

Lock the lid in place and close the seal valve. Press the Cancel button. Press the Manual button to set the cook time for 10 minutes. When the cook time ends, use a natural pressure release for 2 minutes, then a quick pressure release.

When the valve drops, carefully remove the lid. Place the chicken on a cutting board. Let rest for 3 to 5 minutes before chopping. Discard the liquid in the pot.

In a medium bowl, stir together the water chestnuts, raisins, mayonnaise, lemon juice, red onion, cumin, salt, cayenne, and remaining 1 teaspoon of curry powder. Add the chicken. Stir until well coated in the dressing. Cover and refrigerate for 1 hour to allow the flavors to absorb and for the curry to turn a soft yellow color.

Serve the salad with the melon slices.

NUTRITION FACTS

PER SERVING (275 G)

CALORIES 310

		% DAILY VALUE
TOTAL FAT	11G	14%
SATURATED FAT	1G	5%
TRANS FAT	0G	
CHOLESTEROL	65MG	22%
SODIUM	340MG	15%
TOTAL CARBOHYDRATE	31G	11%
DIETARY FIBER	2G	7%
TOTAL SUGARS	22G	
ADDED SUGARS	0G	
PROTEIN 23G		
VITAMIN D	0MCG	
CALCIUM	48MG	4%
IRON	2MG	10%
POTASSIUM	837MG	20%

Lemon-Mint Chicken Couscous Salad

SERVES 4: 1¼ CUPS (330 G) PER SERVING

2 cups (480 ml) water, plus more as needed

¾ cup (129 g) whole-wheat pearl couscous

1 pound (454 g) chicken tenders

2 teaspoons dried oregano leaves, divided

3 tablespoons (27 g) capers

3 ounces (85 g) crumbled reduced-fat feta cheese

½ cup (32 g) chopped fresh mint

½ cup (30 g) chopped fresh parsley

1 cup (135 g) chopped cucumber

Zest of 1 lemon

Juice of 1 lemon

1 tablespoon (15 ml) extra-virgin olive oil

1 garlic clove, minced

1 tablespoon (15 ml) apple cider vinegar

¼ teaspoon salt

1 lemon, quartered

In your pressure cooker cooking pot, combine the water and couscous, making sure the water covers the couscous. Top with the chicken tenders. Sprinkle with 1 teaspoon of oregano.

Lock the lid in place and close the seal valve. Press the Manual button to set the cook time for 4 minutes. When the cook time ends, use a quick pressure release.

When the valve drops, carefully remove the lid. Transfer the chicken to a cutting board and let rest for 3 to 5 minutes. Using a fine-mesh sieve, drain the couscous and run it under cold water to stop the cooking and cool it quickly. Place the couscous in a large bowl. Add the remaining ingredients through the salt, and including the other teaspoon of oregano. Stir to combine.

Chop the chicken and add it to the couscous mixture. Cover and refrigerate for at least 1 hour before serving with the lemon wedges alongside for squeezing.

NUTRITION FACTS

PER SERVING (330 G)

CALORIES	310	
	% DAILY VALUE	
TOTAL FAT	7G	9%
SATURATED FAT	2G	10%
TRANS FAT	0G	
CHOLESTEROL	50MG	17%
SODIUM	610MG	27%
TOTAL CARBOHYDRATE	32G	12%
DIETARY FIBER	1G	4%
TOTAL SUGARS	1G	
ADDED SUGARS	0G	
PROTEIN	30G	
VITAMIN D	0MCG	
CALCIUM	92MG	8%
IRON	3MG	15%
POTASSIUM	104MG	2%

Fresh Lemon-Ginger Salmon Salad

SERVES 4: 2 CUPS SALAD (225 G) PLUS 2 TABLESPOONS (30 ML) DRESSING PER SERVING

FOR SALAD

1 cup (240 ml) water

2 frozen salmon fillets
(6 ounces, or 170 g, each)

½ lemon

¼ teaspoon black pepper

6 cups (426 g) spring greens

1 avocado, peeled, pitted, and chopped

¼ cup (40 g) finely chopped red onion

1 jalapeño pepper, halved lengthwise,
seeded, and thinly sliced

FOR DRESSING

2 tablespoons (25 g) sugar

2 teaspoons grated lemon zest

¼ cup (60 ml) fresh lemon juice

2 tablespoons (30 ml) canola oil

1 tablespoon (8 g) grated peeled fresh ginger

½ teaspoon salt

To make the salad: Add the water to the pressure cooker cooking pot and place the steamer basket inside the pot. Place the salmon in the steamer basket. Squeeze the lemon half over the fish and sprinkle with the pepper.

Lock the lid in place and close the seal valve. Press the Manual button to set the cook time for 4 minutes. When the cook time ends, use a quick pressure release.

When the valve drops, carefully remove the lid. Transfer the salmon to a plate and let cool for about 15 minutes.

Arrange equal amounts of spring greens on each of 4 dinner plates. Flake the salmon and place equal amounts on top of each salad. Top each with one-fourth of the avocado, 1 tablespoon (10 g) of red onion, and one-fourth of the jalapeño.

To make the dressing: In a small bowl, whisk the dressing ingredients until well blended. Spoon 2 tablespoons (30 ml) over each salad.

NUTRITION FACTS

PER SERVING (235 G)

CALORIES	280	
	% DAILY VALUE	
TOTAL FAT	17G	22%
SATURATED FAT	2G	10%
TRANS FAT	0G	
CHOLESTEROL	45MG	15%
SODIUM	390MG	17%
TOTAL CARBOHYDRATE	15G	5%
DIETARY FIBER	4G	14%
TOTAL SUGARS	7G	
ADDED SUGARS	6G	12%
PROTEIN	20G	
VITAMIN D	0MCG	
CALCIUM	63MG	4%
IRON	3MG	15%
POTASSIUM	211MG	4%

Fresh Cucumber, Feta, Lentil Salad

SERVES 4: 1¼ CUPS (154 G) PER SERVING

¾ cup (144 g) dried green or brown lentils, rinsed

2 cups (480 ml) water

1 cup (135 g) chopped cucumber

1 cup (149 g) grape tomatoes, quartered

4 ounces (115 g) crumbled reduced-fat feta cheese

½ cup (32 g) chopped fresh mint

¼ cup (40 g) finely chopped red onion

¼ cup (15 g) chopped fresh parsley

3 tablespoons (45 ml) red wine vinegar

2 tablespoons (30 ml) extra-virgin olive oil

½ teaspoon salt

⅛ teaspoon to ¼ teaspoon red pepper flakes

In your pressure cooker cooking pot, combine the lentils and water.

Lock the lid in place and close the seal valve. Press the Manual button to set the cook time for 7 minutes. When the cook time ends, use a quick pressure release.

When the valve drops, carefully remove the lid. Transfer the lentils to a colander to drain and run under cold water to stop the cooking and cool them quickly.

Meanwhile, in a medium bowl, combine the remaining ingredients and stir to combine. Add the cooled lentils and toss until well blended. Cover and refrigerate for 1 hour before serving.

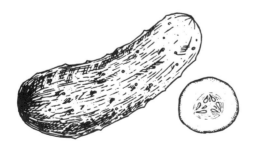

NUTRITION FACTS

PER SERVING (154 G)

CALORIES	270	
	% DAILY VALUE	
TOTAL FAT	11G	14%
SATURATED FAT	3G	15%
TRANS FAT	0G	
CHOLESTEROL	10MG	3%
SODIUM	650MG	28%
TOTAL CARBOHYDRATE	25G	9%
DIETARY FIBER	6G	21%
TOTAL SUGARS	3G	
ADDED SUGARS	0G	
PROTEIN	14G	
VITAMIN D	0MCG	
CALCIUM	102MG	8%
IRON	3MG	15%
POTASSIUM	488MG	10%

Fiesta Bright Rice Salad

SERVES 4: 1¼ CUPS (296 G) PER SERVING

1¼ cups (300 ml) water

1 cup (185 g) uncooked long-grain white rice, rinsed

1 jalapeño pepper, seeded and finely chopped

¼ teaspoon ground turmeric

1½ cups (270 g) chopped tomato

1 avocado, peeled, pitted, and chopped

½ cup (50 g) chopped celery

¼ cup (40 g) chopped red onion

2 tablespoons (30 ml) apple cider vinegar

2 teaspoons extra-virgin olive oil

1 teaspoon salt

½ teaspoon ground cumin

2 ounces (55 g) shredded reduced-fat Mexican cheese blend or sharp white Cheddar cheese

¼ cup (4 g) chopped fresh cilantro (optional)

In your pressure cooker cooking pot, combine the water, rice, jalapeño, and turmeric.

Lock the lid in place and close the seal valve. Press the Manual button to set the cook time for 4 minutes. When the cook time ends, use a natural pressure release for 10 minutes, then a quick pressure release.

When the valve drops, carefully remove the lid. Transfer the cooked rice onto a sheet of aluminum foil or a baking sheet in a thin layer. Let stand for 10 minutes to cool completely.

Meanwhile, in a large bowl combine the tomato, avocado, celery, red onion, vinegar, olive oil, salt, and cumin. Gently stir to combine. Add the cooled rice, cheese, and cilantro (if using). Toss gently until blended.

NUTRITION FACTS

PER SERVING (296 G)

CALORIES	330	
	% DAILY VALUE	
TOTAL FAT	12G	15%
SATURATED FAT	3.5G	18%
TRANS FAT	0G	
CHOLESTEROL	15MG	5%
SODIUM	650MG	28%
TOTAL CARBOHYDRATE	48G	17%
DIETARY FIBER	4G	14%
TOTAL SUGARS	3G	
ADDED SUGARS	0G	
PROTEIN	9G	
VITAMIN D	0MCG	
CALCIUM	128MG	10%
IRON	2MG	10%
POTASSIUM	459MG	10%

NOTE

Brighten up your salad and use ground turmeric when cooking the white rice. The turmeric turns the rice brilliant yellow and makes the other ingredients pop!

Layered Egg and Fresh Crouton Salad Bowls

SERVES 4: ABOUT 2½ CUPS (207 G) SALAD, 3 TABLESPOONS (45 G) DRESSING, PLUS ⅓ CUP (17 G) CROUTONS PER SERVING

1 tablespoon (15 ml) canola oil

2 ounces (55 g) multigrain Italian bread, cut into ½-inch (1 cm) slices, then into ½-inch (1 cm) cubes

1½ teaspoons dried dill, divided

2 cups (480 ml) water

6 large eggs

8 cups (384 g) torn romaine lettuce

¾ cup (180 g) yogurt ranch-style dressing

⅛ teaspoon black pepper

½ cup (80 g) finely chopped red onion

½ cup (65 g) frozen green peas, thawed (see Cook's Note)

⅛ teaspoon salt

NOTE

This will become one of your favorite salads . . . ever. Besides the fact that the peelings literally slip off the cooked eggs, the croutons add another dimension of flavor and crunch . . . and it's made all in one pot! Make more croutons and store them in an airtight container to have on hand, if you like!

On your pressure cooker, select Sauté/Browning + more to preheat the cooking pot. Once hot, add the canola oil to the pot and tilt the pot to coat the bottom lightly. Add the bread cubes in a single layer. Cook for 2 minutes, *without stirring*. Sprinkle with ½ teaspoon dill. Cook for 4 minutes more, stirring occasionally, until they begin to brown. (All sides may not brown evenly.) Transfer to a plate and set aside. Let cool completely to become crisp.

Add the water to the pressure cooker cooking pot and place the steamer basket inside the pot. Place the eggs in the steamer basket.

Lock the lid in place and close the seal valve. Press the Cancel button. Press the Manual button to set the cook time for 6 minutes. When the cook time ends, use a quick pressure release.

Meanwhile, prepare an ice bath in a medium bowl and set aside.

When the valve drops, carefully remove the lid. Using tongs or a large spoon, immediately transfer the eggs to the ice water. Let stand for 1 minute. Peel and slice the eggs.

Arrange equal amounts of romaine lettuce in each of 4 shallow bowls. Top with equal amounts of the egg slices covering the entire surface of the lettuce bowl. Drizzle evenly with the ranch dressing. Sprinkle the salads with remaining 1 teaspoon of dill and the pepper. Top each with 2 tablespoons (20 g) of the red onion and 2 tablespoons (16.25 g) of the green peas. Top with the croutons and sprinkle with the salt.

NUTRITION FACTS

PER SERVING (269 G)

CALORIES 260

	% DAILY VALUE	
TOTAL FAT	16G	21%
SATURATED FAT	3.5G	18%
TRANS FAT	0G	
CHOLESTEROL	285MG	95%
SODIUM	660MG	29%
TOTAL CARBOHYDRATE	17G	6%
DIETARY FIBER	2G	7%
TOTAL SUGARS	6G	
ADDED SUGARS	0G	
PROTEIN	14G	
VITAMIN D	2MCG	10%
CALCIUM	123MG	10%
IRON	3MG	15%
POTASSIUM	365MG	8%

CHAPTER 3

One-Dish Suppers

All-in-one recipes have always been a priority for people on the run, but quite often they are packed with calories, carbs, fat grams, and sodium. The recipes in this section are packed with flavor, protein, and tons of veggies . . . they're family friendly and easy to prep, too!

Chicken and New Potatoes with Lemony Sauce

SERVES 4: 1 CHICKEN THIGH, 3 OUNCES (170 G) POTATOES, AND ABOUT ¼ CUP (60 ML) SAUCE PER SERVING

1 lemon, cut into 8 wedges

6 garlic cloves, peeled

1 cup (240 ml) water

1 teaspoon paprika

½ teaspoon poultry seasoning or 1 teaspoon dried thyme

1 teaspoon onion powder

½ teaspoon black pepper

¾ teaspoon salt, divided

4 bone-in skinless chicken thighs (about 2 pounds, or 908 g, total)

12 ounces (340 g) petite red or Yukon gold potatoes, about 1 inch (2.5 cm) in diameter

NOTE

For a thicker sauce, combine 1 tablespoon (15 ml) cold water and 1 tablespoon (8 g) cornstarch and stir until dissolved. Add to the boiling liquid and boil for 1 minute.

Continued

In your pressure cooker cooking pot, combine the lemon, garlic, and water. In a small bowl, stir together the paprika, poultry seasoning, onion powder, pepper, and ¼ teaspoon of salt. Place the chicken on top of the lemons. Sprinkle with the paprika mixture.

Lock the lid in place and close the seal valve. Press the Manual button to set the cook time for 15 minutes. When the cook time ends, use a quick pressure release.

When the valve drops, carefully remove the lid. Remove the chicken and lemons from the pot and place them on a serving platter. Cover with aluminum foil to keep warm.

Add the potatoes and remaining ½ teaspoon of salt to the liquid in the pot.

Lock the lid in place and close the seal valve. Press the Cancel button. Press the Manual button to set the cook time for 3 minutes. When the cook time ends, use a quick pressure release.

When the valve drops, carefully remove the lid.

Press the Cancel button. Select Sauté/Browning + more. Bring the liquid to a boil and boil for 5 minutes to thicken the sauce slightly. Spoon the potatoes and sauce over the chicken.

NUTRITION FACTS

PER SERVING (317 G)

CALORIES	340	
	% DAILY VALUE	
TOTAL FAT	9G	12%
SATURATED FAT	2.5G	13%
TRANS FAT	0G	
CHOLESTEROL	215MG	72%
SODIUM	670MG	29%
TOTAL CARBOHYDRATE	15G	5%
DIETARY FIBER	2G	7%
TOTAL SUGARS	1G	
ADDED SUGARS	0G	
PROTEIN	46G	
VITAMIN D	0MCG	
CALCIUM	33MG	2%
IRON	3MG	15%
POTASSIUM	954MG	20%

Spicy Pineapple Chicken and Snow Peas

SERVES 4: 1½ CUPS (314 G) CHICKEN MIXTURE AND VEGETABLES,
2 TABLESPOONS (30 ML) SAUCE, AND 1 TABLESPOON (7 G) PEANUTS PER SERVING

FOR SAUCE

3 tablespoons (45 ml) light soy sauce

2 tablespoons (25 g) sugar

1½ tablespoons (23 ml) apple cider vinegar

2 teaspoons grated peeled fresh ginger

⅛ teaspoon red pepper flakes

FOR CHICKEN

1 ounce (28 g) unsalted peanuts

1 tablespoon (15 ml) canola oil

12 ounces (340 g) boneless, skinless chicken thighs, trimmed and cut into 1-inch (2.5 cm) cubes

1 cup (160 g) coarsely chopped onion

2 (8-ounce, or 225 g) cans pineapple chunks in their own juice

½ teaspoon curry powder

¼ teaspoon salt

4 ounces (115 g) fresh snow peas, trimmed

1 medium red bell pepper, thinly sliced

NOTE

No need for rice here. The combination of chicken and pineapple surrounded by snow peas and peppers, topped with a sweet ginger soy sauce and peanuts, is definitely all that's needed . . . and all done in one pot!

Continued

To make the sauce: In a small bowl, whisk all the sauce ingredients to combine and set aside.

To make the chicken: On your pressure cooker, select Sauté/Browning + more to preheat the cooking pot. Once hot, add the peanuts to the pot. Cook for 4 minutes, or until beginning to lightly brown. Remove from the pot and set aside.

Add the canola oil and tilt the pot to coat the bottom lightly. Add the chicken. Do not stir. Cook for 5 minutes. Add the onion, pineapple and juice, curry powder, and salt. Stir to blend.

Lock the lid in place and close the seal valve. Press the Cancel button. Press the Manual button to set the cook time for 4 minutes. Quick release. When the valve drops, carefully remove the lid. Using a slotted spoon, transfer the ingredients to a rimmed platter or shallow pasta bowl. Cover to keep warm.

Add the snow peas and red bell pepper to the liquid in pot.

Lock the lid in place and close the seal valve. Press the Cancel button. Press the Manual button to set the cook time for 1 minute. When the cook time ends, use a quick pressure release.

When the valve drops, carefully remove the lid. Using a slotted spoon, remove the vegetables and arrange them around the chicken mixture. Drizzle the sauce over the chicken mixture, and sprinkle with the peanuts.

NUTRITION FACTS

SERVING SIZE (351 G)		
CALORIES	340	
	% DAILY VALUE	
TOTAL FAT	13G	17%
SATURATED FAT	2.5G	13%
TRANS FAT	0G	
CHOLESTEROL	55MG	18%
SODIUM	630MG	27%
TOTAL CARBOHYDRATE	33G	12%
DIETARY FIBER	4G	14%
TOTAL SUGARS	26G	
ADDED SUGARS	6G	12%
PROTEIN	21G	
VITAMIN D	0MCG	
CALCIUM	37MG	2%
IRON	2MG	10%
POTASSIUM	562MG	10%

Cheesy Chicken and Poblano Rice

SERVES 4: 1¼ CUPS (300 G) PER SERVING

1 teaspoon canola oil

2 cups (236 g) chopped poblano chile (from about 4 chiles)

12 ounces (340 g) boneless skinless chicken breast, cut into bite-size pieces

¾ cup (139 g) long-grain white rice, rinsed

¾ cup (180 ml) water

2 teaspoons ground cumin, divided

¼ teaspoon ground turmeric

3 ounces (85 g) shredded reduced-fat Mexican cheese blend

¾ teaspoon salt

¼ teaspoon pepper

On your pressure cooker, select Sauté/Browning + more to preheat the cooking pot. Once hot, add the canola oil and tilt the pot to coat the bottom lightly. Add the poblanos. Cook for 8 minutes, stirring occasionally. (Note: Do not stir often, you want a "roasted" pepper effect.) Add the chicken in a single layer. Cook for 2 minutes *without stirring*.

Stir in the rice, water, 1 teaspoon of cumin, and the turmeric.

Lock the lid in place and close the seal valve. Press the Cancel button. Press the Manual button to set the cook time for 4 minutes. When the cook time ends, use a natural pressure release for 10 minutes, then a quick pressure release.

When the valve drops, carefully remove the lid. Stir in the remaining 1 teaspoon of cumin, the cheese, salt, and pepper.

NUTRITION FACTS

PER SERVING (300 G)		
CALORIES	350	
	% DAILY VALUE	
TOTAL FAT	8G	10%
SATURATED FAT	3.5G	18%
TRANS FAT	0G	
CHOLESTEROL	75MG	25%
SODIUM	630MG	27%
TOTAL CARBOHYDRATE	39G	14%
DIETARY FIBER	2G	7%
TOTAL SUGARS	4G	
ADDED SUGARS	0G	
PROTEIN 30G		
VITAMIN D	0MCG	
CALCIUM	220MG	15%
IRON	3MG	15%
POTASSIUM	611MG	15%

Chicken and Wild Rice Pilaf

SERVES 4: 1 CUP (242 G) PER SERVING

Nonstick cooking spray, for preparing the cooking pot

⅔ cup (107 g) wild rice

⅓ cup (63 g) brown rice

1½ cups (360 ml) fat-free reduced-sodium chicken broth

1½ cups (360 ml) water

8 ounces (225 g) boneless skinless chicken breast, chopped

1½ ounces (43 g) roasted hulled pumpkin seeds

¼ cup (40 g) dried cherries

¼ cup (25 g) chopped scallion

1 tablespoon (15 ml) extra-virgin olive oil

½ teaspoon poultry seasoning

½ teaspoon salt

In your pressure cooker cooking pot, combine the wild rice, brown rice, chicken broth, and water.

Lock the lid in place and close the seal valve. Press the Manual button to set the cook time for 20 minutes. When the cook time ends, use a quick pressure release.

When the valve drops, carefully remove the lid. In a fine-mesh sieve, drain the rice mixture and set aside.

Press the Cancel button. Select Sauté/Browning + more and coat the pot with cooking spray. Add the chicken. Cook for 3 minutes, or until the chicken is no longer pink in the center, stirring occasionally. Turn off the pressure cooker. Stir in the drained rice mixture and the remaining ingredients.

NUTRITION FACTS

PER SERVING (242 G)

CALORIES	330	
	% DAILY VALUE	
TOTAL FAT	11G	14%
SATURATED FAT	2G	10%
TRANS FAT	0G	
CHOLESTEROL	40MG	13%
SODIUM	510MG	22%
TOTAL CARBOHYDRATE	40G	15%
DIETARY FIBER	4G	14%
TOTAL SUGARS	7G	
ADDED SUGARS	0G	
PROTEIN	21G	
VITAMIN D	0MCG	
CALCIUM	25MG	2%
IRON	2MG	10%
POTASSIUM	467MG	10%

Cheddar Potato, Edamame, and Fennel Casserole

SERVES 4: 1½ CUPS (265 G) PER SERVING

⅓ cup (17 g) panko bread crumbs

1 cup (240 ml) water

1¼ pounds (567.5 g) red potatoes, cut into ¼-inch (0.6 cm)-thick slices

1 cup (85 g) thinly sliced fennel bulb

1 cup (150 g) fresh or frozen shelled edamame

¼ cup (60 ml) 2% milk

1½ teaspoons cornstarch

1 teaspoon garlic powder

1 teaspoon dried oregano

½ teaspoon dried thyme

¾ teaspoon salt

¼ teaspoon black pepper

5 ounces (140 g) shredded reduced-fat sharp Cheddar cheese

On your pressure cooker, select Sauté/Browning + more to preheat the cooking pot. Once hot, add the bread crumbs to the pot. Cook for 3 minutes, or until beginning to lightly brown, stirring occasionally. Transfer to a plate and set aside.

Put a steamer basket into the pot and pour in the water. Place the potatoes, fennel, and edamame in the basket.

Lock the lid in place and close the seal valve. Press the Cancel button. Press the Manual button to set the cook time for 2 minutes. When the cook time ends, use a quick pressure release.

When the valve drops, carefully remove the lid. Press the Cancel button. Select Sauté/Browning + more. Remove the vegetable mixture and the steamer basket. Place the vegetables in a shallow casserole dish.

In a small bowl, whisk the milk and cornstarch. Add this slurry to the liquid in the pot and bring to a boil. Boil for 1 minute, or until slightly thickened.

Stir in the garlic powder, oregano, thyme, salt, and pepper. Gradually add the cheese, stirring until melted and smooth. Pour the cheese sauce over the potato mixture in the casserole dish and gently toss to distribute the sauce evenly. Top with the bread crumbs. Let stand for 15 minutes to let the cheese to melt and the flavors absorb.

NUTRITION FACTS

SERVING SIZE (265 G)		
CALORIES	290	
		% DAILY VALUE
TOTAL FAT	9G	12%
SATURATED FAT	5G	25%
TRANS FAT	0G	
CHOLESTEROL	30MG	10%
SODIUM	730MG	32%
TOTAL CARBOHYDRATE	36G	13%
DIETARY FIBER	5G	18%
TOTAL SUGARS	4G	
ADDED SUGARS	0G	
PROTEIN	18G	
VITAMIN D	0MCG	
CALCIUM	358MG	30%
IRON	2MG	10%
POTASSIUM	806MG	15%

Shepherd's Pie in a Pot

SERVES 4: 1½ CUPS (450 G) PER SERVING

Nonstick cooking spray, for preparing the cooking pot

12 ounces (340 g) 93% lean ground turkey

1 zucchini, cut into ½-inch (1 cm) cubes

2 teaspoons chili powder

2 teaspoons light soy sauce

3½ cups (840 ml) water, divided

½ teaspoon salt, divided

¼ teaspoon black pepper, divided

1 pound (454 g) red potatoes, cut into ½-inch (1 cm) cubes

¾ cup (180 ml) nonfat evaporated milk

2 ounces (55 g) shredded reduced-fat sharp Cheddar cheese

NOTE

This is a fun and fast way to make a family favorite . . . upside-down! Sauté the turkey mixture in the pot first then cook and mash the potatoes (in the pot) and finish the dish by topping with the turkey and the cheese . . . all done in one pot and waiting to be scooped onto your plate.

On your pressure cooker, select Sauté/Browning + more to preheat the cooking pot. Once hot, coat the pot with cooking spray. Add the ground turkey. Cook for 4 minutes, or until beginning to lightly brown, stirring occasionally. Add the zucchini, chili powder, soy sauce, ½ cup (120 ml) of water, ⅛ teaspoon of salt, and ⅛ teaspoon of pepper. Cook for 2 minutes, or until the zucchini is just crisp-tender. Transfer the mixture into a bowl and cover with aluminum foil to keep warm.

Add the remaining 3 cups (720 ml) of water to the pressure cooker cooking pot and place a steamer basket inside the pot. Place the potatoes in the steamer basket.

Lock the lid in place and close the seal valve. Press the Cancel button. Press the Manual button to set the cook time for 5 minutes. When the cook time ends, use a quick pressure release.

When the valve drops, carefully remove the lid. Turn off the pressure cooker. Remove the potatoes and steamer basket from the pot. Discard the water and return the potatoes to the pot. Using a potato masher or handheld electric mixer, mash the potatoes in the pot. Add the evaporated milk and mash until well blended. (They may be a little thick at this point.) Season with the remaining ⅜ teaspoon of salt and ⅛ teaspoon of pepper. Spoon the turkey mixture and any accumulated juices evenly over the potatoes. Sprinkle with the cheese.

Select Sauté/Browning + more. Cook, uncovered, for 2 to 3 minutes, or until the mixture *just* comes to a boil around the outer edges of the potatoes. Immediately turn off the pressure cooker and, wearing oven mitts, transfer the cooking pot to a heatproof surface. Let rest for 5 minutes, uncovered, to allow the cheese to melt and to thicken slightly.

NUTRITION FACTS

PER SERVING (308 G)

CALORIES	300	
	% DAILY VALUE	
TOTAL FAT	11G	14%
SATURATED FAT	4G	20%
TRANS FAT	0G	
CHOLESTEROL	75MG	25%
SODIUM	650MG	28%
TOTAL CARBOHYDRATE	26G	9%
DIETARY FIBER	3G	11%
TOTAL SUGARS	8G	
ADDED SUGARS	0G	
PROTEIN	26G	
VITAMIN D	1MCG	6%
CALCIUM	287MG	20%
IRON	2MG	10%
POTASSIUM	1,002MG	20%

Burgundy Beef with Sweet Potato Mash

SERVES 4: 1 CUP (276 G) BEEF MIXTURE AND
ABOUT ½ CUP (124 G) SWEET POTATOES PER SERVING

Nonstick cooking spray, for preparing the cooking pot

1 pound (454 g) boneless beef chuck, cut into 1-inch (2.5 cm) cubes

2 (0.14-ounce, or 4 g) packets sodium-free beef bouillon granules

1 (8-ounce, or 225 g) can tomato sauce

⅓ cup (80 ml) dry red wine

¼ cup (60 ml) water

1½ cups (225 g) chopped red bell pepper

¾ cup (120 g) chopped onion

1 bay leaf

½ teaspoon garlic powder

½ teaspoon black pepper

½ teaspoon sugar

¼ teaspoon red pepper flakes

1 (24-ounce, or 680 g) package mashed sweet potatoes (such as Simply Potatoes)

On your pressure cooker, select Sauté/Browning + more to preheat the cooking pot. Once hot, coat the pot with cooking spray. Add half the beef. Cook for 5 minutes, without stirring.

Add the remaining half of the beef and the bouillon granules, tomato sauce, red wine, water, red bell pepper, onion, bay leaf, garlic powder, black pepper, sugar, and red pepper flakes. Stir to blend.

Lock the lid in place and close the seal valve. Press the Cancel button. Press the Manual button to set the cook time for 30 minutes. When the cook time ends, use a natural pressure release.

When the valve drops, carefully remove the lid. Using a slotted spoon, transfer the beef to a plate.

Press the Cancel button. Select Sauté/Browning + more. Bring the liquid in the pot to a boil. Cook for 7 minutes, or until reduced to 1½ cups (360 ml). Return the beef to the pot and cook for 1 minute to heat through.

Meanwhile, prepare the sweet potatoes according to the package directions. Serve the beef and sauce over the sweet potatoes.

NUTRITION FACTS

SERVING SIZE (400 G)		
CALORIES	350	
	% DAILY VALUE	
TOTAL FAT	6G	8%
SATURATED FAT	1.5G	8%
TRANS FAT	0G	
CHOLESTEROL	45MG	15%
SODIUM	650MG	28%
TOTAL CARBOHYDRATE	42G	15%
DIETARY FIBER	3G	11%
TOTAL SUGARS	25G	
ADDED SUGARS	1G	2%
PROTEIN	26G	
VITAMIN D	0MCG	
CALCIUM	108MG	8%
IRON	4MG	20%
POTASSIUM	365MG	8%

Sausage Pepper Pasta Pot

SERVES 4: 1½ CUPS (300 G) PER SERVING

Nonstick cooking spray, for preparing the cooking pot

8 ounces (225 g) Italian turkey sausage

2 large green bell peppers, cut into 1-inch (2.5 cm) pieces

4 ounces (115 g) sliced mushrooms

4 ounces (115 g) multigrain penne, such as Barilla Plus

1 cup (250 g) prepared reduced-sodium spaghetti sauce

1 cup (240 ml) water

1 tablespoon (2 g) dried basil leaves

⅛ teaspoon red pepper flakes (optional)

2 cups (60 g) fresh baby spinach

16 pitted kalamata olives, coarsely chopped

1 tablespoon (15 ml) extra-virgin olive oil

On your pressure cooker, select Sauté/Browning + more to preheat the cooking pot. Once hot, coat the pot with cooking spray. Add the sausages. Cook for 4 minutes, or until beginning to brown, stirring occasionally. Stir in the green bell peppers, mushrooms, pasta, spaghetti sauce, water, basil, and red pepper flakes (if using).

Lock the lid in place and close the seal valve. Press the Cancel button. Press the Manual button to set the cook time for 5 minutes. When the cook time ends, use a quick pressure release.

When the valve drops, carefully remove the lid. Add the spinach and olives. Stir for about 1 minute until the spinach is just wilted. Drizzle in the olive oil. Let stand, uncovered, for 2 minutes to thicken slightly and so the flavors blend.

NUTRITION FACTS

PER SERVING (300 G)		
CALORIES	320	
	% DAILY VALUE	
TOTAL FAT	15G	19%
SATURATED FAT	2G	10%
TRANS FAT	0G	
CHOLESTEROL	30MG	10%
SODIUM	800MG	35%
TOTAL CARBOHYDRATE	32G	12%
DIETARY FIBER	2G	7%
TOTAL SUGARS	8G	
ADDED SUGARS	0G	
PROTEIN	17G	
VITAMIN D	0MCG	
CALCIUM	65MG	6%
IRON	3MG	15%
POTASSIUM	410MG	8%

Louisiana Sausage and Pepper "Dirty" Rice

SERVES 4: 1 CUP (231 G) PER SERVING

Nonstick cooking spray, for preparing the cooking pot

3-ounce (85 g) pork andouille sausage link (such as Aidells), finely chopped

8 ounces (225 g) lean ground beef

½ cup (75 g) finely chopped green bell pepper

½ cup (75 g) finely chopped red bell pepper

½ cup (50 g) finely chopped scallion

1 cup (185 g) long-grain white rice, rinsed

1¼ cups (300 ml) water

2 teaspoons seafood seasoning, such as Old Bay

¼ cup (15 g) chopped fresh parsley

On your pressure cooker, select Sauté/ Browning + more to preheat the cooking pot. Once hot, coat the pot with cooking spray. Add the sausage and ground beef. Cook for 3 minutes, or until beginning to lightly brown, stirring frequently. Stir in the green and red bell peppers, scallion, rice, water, and seafood seasoning.

Lock the lid in place and close the seal valve. Press the Cancel button. Press the Manual button to set the cook time for 3 minutes. When the cook time ends, use a natural pressure release.

When the valve drops, carefully remove the lid. Stir in the parsley.

NUTRITION FACTS

PER SERVING (231 G)

CALORIES	320	
	% DAILY VALUE	
TOTAL FAT	7G	9%
SATURATED FAT	3G	15%
TRANS FAT	0G	
CHOLESTEROL	50MG	17%
SODIUM 660MG	29%	
TOTAL CARBOHYDRATE	44G	16%
DIETARY FIBER	2G	7%
TOTAL SUGARS	2G	
ADDED SUGARS	0G	
PROTEIN	20G	
VITAMIN D	0MCG	
CALCIUM	33MG	2%
IRON	2MG	10%
POTASSIUM	178MG	4%

Asian Two-Grain Bowl

SERVES 4: 1¼ CUPS RICE MIXTURE (255 G), 2 TABLESPOONS (13.75 G) NUTS, AND 2 TABLESPOONS (30 ML) SAUCE PER SERVING

FOR SAUCE

¼ cup (60 ml) light soy sauce

2 tablespoons (30 ml) fresh lime juice

2 tablespoons (25 g) sugar

1 teaspoon grated peeled fresh ginger

⅛ teaspoon red pepper flakes

FOR BASE

2 ounces (55 g) slivered almonds

½ cup (93 g) basmati rice

½ cup (92 g) quinoa

1½ cups (360 ml) water

1 cup (148 g) fresh shelled edamame or frozen, thawed

4 medium scallions, chopped

1 cup (150 g) chopped yellow bell pepper

NOTE

Looking for ways to add more fiber and protein to your diet? Try quinoa. If you're unfamiliar with this grain, a nice way to introduce yourself to it is combined with another grain, such as rice . . . then you'll be hooked!

To make the sauce: In a small bowl, whisk together the sauce ingredients until combined. Set aside.

To make the base: On your pressure cooker, select Sauté/Browning + more to preheat the cooking pot. Once hot, add the almonds. Cook for 4 minutes, or until beginning to lightly brown, stirring occasionally. Transfer to a plate and set aside.

Place the rice and quinoa into the pot. Carefully add the water.

Lock the lid in place and close the seal valve. Press the Cancel button. Press the Manual button to set the cook time for 4 minutes. When the cook time ends, use a quick pressure release.

When the valve drops, carefully remove the lid. Stir in the edamame, scallions, and yellow bell pepper. Cover the pot and let stand for 2 minutes.

Stir the sauce and spoon it over the rice mixture. Sprinkle with the toasted almonds.

NUTRITION FACTS

PER SERVING (255 G)		
CALORIES	330	
	% DAILY VALUE	
TOTAL FAT	10G	13%
SATURATED FAT	0.5G	3%
TRANS FAT	0G	
CHOLESTEROL	0MG	
SODIUM	590MG	26%
TOTAL CARBOHYDRATE	46G	17%
DIETARY FIBER	5G	18%
TOTAL SUGARS	5G	
ADDED SUGARS	2G	4%
PROTEIN	13G	
VITAMIN D	0MCG	
CALCIUM	76MG	6%
IRON	3MG	15%
POTASSIUM	310MG	6%

Middle Eastern Spiced Tomato Couscous

SERVES 4: 1 CUP (275 G) PER SERVING

1 teaspoon canola oil

½ cup (80 g) finely chopped onion

½ cup (55 g) slivered almonds or (68 g) pine nuts

1 can (14.5-ounces, or 410 g) stewed tomatoes

½ cup (86 g) pearl couscous

¾ cup (180 ml) water

½ cup (114 g) pimiento-stuffed olives

⅓ cup (50 g) raisins

1 teaspoon ground cumin

⅛ teaspoon cayenne pepper

½ can (15 ounces, or 425 g) no-salt-added chickpeas, rinsed and drained

⅓ cup (5 g) chopped fresh cilantro

2 teaspoons grated peeled fresh ginger

¼ teaspoon salt

On your pressure cooker, select Sauté/Browning + more to preheat the cooking pot. Once hot, add the canola oil and tilt the pot to coat the bottom lightly. Add the onion and almonds. Cook for 5 minutes until lightly browned, stirring frequently. Stir in the tomatoes, couscous, water, olives, raisins, cumin, and cayenne.

Lock the lid in place and close the seal valve. Press the Cancel button. Press the Manual button to set the cook time for 4 minutes. When the cook time ends, use a quick pressure release.

When the valve drops, carefully remove the lid. Stir in the chickpeas, cilantro, ginger, and salt, breaking up any larger pieces of tomato that remain with a fork. Cover, do not lock the lid, and let stand for 5 minutes to absorb the flavors and allow the couscous to continue cooking.

NUTRITION FACTS

PER SERVING(275 G)

CALORIES	290	
	% DAILY VALUE	
TOTAL FAT	11G	14%
SATURATED FAT	0.5G	3%
TRANS FAT	0G	
CHOLESTEROL	0MG	
SODIUM	630MG	27%
TOTAL CARBOHYDRATE	40G	15%
DIETARY FIBER	3G	11%
TOTAL SUGARS	12G	
ADDED SUGARS	0G	
PROTEIN	8G	
VITAMIN D	0MCG	
CALCIUM	81MG	6%
IRON	2MG	10%
POTASSIUM	283MG	6%

NOTE

For a thinner consistency, after letting stand for 5 minutes, add ¼ to ⅓ cup (60 to 80 ml) of water.

Two-Cheese Cauliflower Rotini

SERVES 4: 1 CUP (210 G) PER SERVING

4 ounces (115 g) multigrain rotini, such as Barilla Plus

1½ cups (360 ml) water, plus more as needed

2 cups (200 g) small (about 1-inch, 2.5 cm) cauliflower florets

¼ cup (60 ml) 2% milk

1 teaspoon cornstarch

½ teaspoon Dijon mustard

1 small red bell pepper, cut in into thin strips, about 2 inches (5 cm) long

½ teaspoon salt

Pinch of cayenne pepper

3 ounces (85 g) reduced-fat sharp white or yellow Cheddar cheese, shredded

1 ounce (28 g) sliced Swiss cheese, torn into small pieces

Black pepper, to taste

In your pressure cooker cooking pot, combine the rotini and water, making sure all the pasta is covered with water.

Lock the lid in place and close the seal valve. Press the Manual button to set the cook time for 3 minutes. When the cook time ends, use a quick pressure release.

When the valve drops, carefully remove the lid. Stir in the cauliflower.

In a small bowl, whisk the milk, cornstarch, and mustard until the cornstarch dissolves. Stir this slurry mixture into the cauliflower mixture.

Press the Cancel button. Select Sauté/Browning + more. Bring the mixture to a boil. Cook, uncovered, for 4 minutes, or until the cauliflower is just crisp-tender, stirring occasionally. Turn off the pressure cooker. Stir in the red bell pepper, salt, and cayenne until well blended. Gradually add the cheeses, stirring to combine. Sprinkle with the black pepper.

NUTRITION FACTS

PER SERVING (210 G)		
CALORIES	220	
	% DAILY VALUE	
TOTAL FAT	8G	10%
SATURATED FAT	4.5G	23%
TRANS FAT	0G	
CHOLESTEROL	20MG	7%
SODIUM	570MG	25%
TOTAL CARBOHYDRATE	24G	9%
DIETARY FIBER	1G	4%
TOTAL SUGARS	3G	
ADDED SUGARS	0G	
PROTEIN	13G	
VITAMIN D	0MCG	
CALCIUM	252MG	20%
IRON	2MG	10%
POTASSIUM	167MG	4%

NOTE

For a thinner consistency, add 1 to 2 tablespoons (15 to 30 ml) more milk at the end.

Warm Quinoa and Kale Black Bean Bowls

SERVES 4: 1 CUP (75 G) BEAN MIXTURE, 1 TABLESPOON (15 ML) SAUCE
AND ABOUT ¼ CUP (36.5 G) AVOCADO PER SERVING

4 ounces (115 g) dried black beans, rinsed

4 cups (960 ml) water

½ cup (92 g) quinoa

2 cups (85 g) baby kale mix

1 jalapeño pepper, seeded and minced

2 tablespoons (30 ml) extra-virgin olive oil

2 tablespoons (30 ml) fresh lemon juice

1 garlic clove, minced

¾ teaspoon salt

1 avocado, peeled, pitted, and chopped

NOTE

Deep dark black beans are cooked with quinoa, served with a warm jalapeño-citrus oil, and topped with chunks of avocado. A striking presentation. This can be served in4 individual shallow bowls, if desired,either hot or cold.

Continued

In your pressure cooker cooking pot, combine the black beans and water.

Lock the lid in place and close the seal valve. Press the Manual button to set the cook time for 18 minutes. When the cook time ends, use a quick pressure release.

When the valve drops, carefully remove the lid. Stir in the quinoa.

Lock the lid in place and close the seal valve. Press the Cancel button. Press the Manual button to set the cook time for 1 minute. When the cook time ends, use a quick pressure release.

When the valve drops, carefully remove the lid. Drain the bean mixture in a fine-mesh sieve (not a colander), discarding the liquid. Place the bean mixture in a shallow bowl. Add the kale mix. Toss until well blended.

In a small bowl, whisk the jalapeño, olive oil, lemon juice, garlic, and salt.

Press the Cancel button. Select Sauté/Browning + more. Pour the jalapeño mixture into the cooking pot and bring it to a boil. Cook for 1 minute, or until it reduces to ¼ cup (60 ml). Spoon the liquid evenly over the bean mixture. Do NOT stir, and top with the avocado.

NUTRITION FACTS

PER SERVING (126 G)

CALORIES	340	
		% DAILY VALUE
TOTAL FAT	17G	22%
SATURATED FAT	2.5G	13%
TRANS FAT	0G	
CHOLESTEROL	0MG	
SODIUM	450MG	20%
TOTAL CARBOHYDRATE	38G	14%
DIETARY FIBER	5G	18%
TOTAL SUGARS	5G	
ADDED SUGARS	0G	
PROTEIN	10G	
VITAMIN D	0MCG	
CALCIUM	98MG	8%
IRON	4MG	20%
POTASSIUM	796MG	15%

Broccoli Walnut Rice Bowls

SERVES 4: 1⅓ CUPS (226 G) PER SERVING

Nonstick cooking spray, for preparing the cooking pot

1 cup (160 g) chopped onion

1⅓ cups (320 ml) water

1 cup (190 g) brown rice

2 garlic cloves, sliced lengthwise

2 cups (142 g) small (about 1-inch, or 2.5 cm) broccoli florets

3 ounces (85 g) chopped walnuts

¼ teaspoon salt

2 tablespoons (30 ml) light soy sauce

1 teaspoon sesame oil

1½ teaspoons Sriracha

On your pressure cooker, select Sauté/Browning + more to preheat the cooking pot. Once hot, coat the pot with cooking spray. Add the onion and coat it with cooking spray. Cook for 10 minutes, or until beginning to richly brown, stirring occasionally. Transfer to a plate and set aside.

Add the water, rice, and garlic to the pot.

Lock the lid in place and close the seal valve. Press the Cancel button. Press the Manual button to set the cook time for 22 minutes. When the cook time ends, use a natural pressure release for 10 minutes, then use a quick pressure release.

When the valve drops, carefully remove the lid. Stir in the broccoli. Cover the pot and let stand for 4 minutes.

Stir in the cooked onion, walnuts, and salt. Divide the rice among 4 individual bowls. Spoon the soy sauce evenly over each. Drizzle evenly with the sesame oil and Sriracha.

NUTRITION FACTS

PER SERVING (226 G)

CALORIES 350

		% DAILY VALUE
TOTAL FAT	17G	22%
SATURATED FAT	2G	10%
TRANS FAT	0G	
CHOLESTEROL	0MG	
SODIUM	500MG	22%
TOTAL CARBOHYDRATE	44G	16%
DIETARY FIBER	4G	14%
TOTAL SUGARS	3G	
ADDED SUGARS	0G	
PROTEIN	9G	
VITAMIN D	0MCG	
CALCIUM	48MG	4%
IRON	2MG	10%
POTASSIUM	362MG	8%

Fall-Apart Pot Roast and Vegetables

SERVES 6: ABOUT 3 OUNCES (85 G) COOKED BEEF, 1½ CUPS (223 G)
VEGETABLES, AND ¼ CUP (60 ML) GRAVY PER SERVING

3 tablespoons (24 g) all-purpose flour

1 tablespoon (15 ml) canola oil

2-pounds (908 g) boneless lean beef chuck roast, about 2½ inches (6 cm) thick, trimmed of fat, patted dry with paper towels

2 cups (182 g) frozen pepper stir-fry

2 celery stalks, cut into 2-inch (5 cm) pieces

1⅓ cups (320 ml) water, divided

1 bay leaf

2 tablespoons (30 g) ketchup

2 packets (0.14 ounce, or 4 g, each) sodium-free beef bouillon granules

1 teaspoon instant coffee granules

1¼ teaspoons salt, divided

½ teaspoon black pepper, divided

1½ pounds (679 g) petite potatoes, halved

1½ pounds (679 g) carrots, cut into 2-inch (5 cm) pieces

NOTE

Browning the flour initially gives the gravy a deep, rich flavor. It ties the whole dish together, giving it that home-cooked taste (but without the added fat grams!). If you want to skip the browning, you can, but the gravy will have a much lighter flavor.

Continued

On your pressure cooker, select Sauté/Browning + more to preheat the cooking pot. Once hot, add the flour to the pot. Cook for 10 minutes, or until pale brown, stirring occasionally. Transfer to a plate and set aside.

Add the oil to the pot and tilt the pot to coat the bottom lightly. Add the beef. Cook for 5 minutes *without turning* to brown one side. Transfer to another plate and set aside.

Add the frozen stir-fry mix, celery, 1 cup (240 ml) of water, and the bay leaf to the pot. Top with the beef (browned-side up). Spread the ketchup over the beef. Sprinkle it with the bouillon granules, coffee granules, 1 teaspoon of salt, and ¼ teaspoon of pepper.

Lock the lid in place and close the seal valve. Press the Cancel button. Press the Manual button to set the cook time for 1 hour, 15 minutes. When the cook time ends, use a quick pressure release.

When the valve drops, carefully remove the lid. Transfer the beef to a serving platter. Cover with aluminum foil.

Add the potatoes and carrots to the pot.

Lock the lid in place and close the seal valve. Press the Cancel button. Press the Manual button to set the cook time for 4 minutes. When the cook time ends, use a quick pressure release. Using a slotted spoon, transfer the vegetables to the platter with the beef, surrounding the beef. Re-cover to keep warm.

In a small bowl, whisk the remaining ⅓ cup (80 ml) of water and the toasted flour until blended. Remove ½ cup (120 ml) of hot liquid from the pot and whisk it into the flour-water mixture until blend well. Add this slurry to the pot along with the remaining ¼ teaspoon of salt and ¼ teaspoon of pepper.

Press the Cancel button. Select Sauté/Browning + more. Bring the liquid in the cooking pot to a boil. Boil for 5 minutes, or until reduced to 1½ cups (360 ml). Spoon gravy over the beef and vegetables.

NUTRITION FACTS

PER SERVING (368 G)		
CALORIES	350	
		% DAILY VALUE
TOTAL FAT	9G	12%
SATURATED FAT	2.5G	13%
TRANS FAT	0G	
CHOLESTEROL	80MG	27%
SODIUM	700MG	30%
TOTAL CARBOHYDRATE	36G	13%
DIETARY FIBER	6G	21%
TOTAL SUGARS	10G	
ADDED SUGARS	1G	2%
PROTEIN	31G	
VITAMIN D	0MCG	
CALCIUM	71MG	6%
IRON	4MG	20%
POTASSIUM	1,157MG	25%

Pork Roast with Root Vegetables au Jus

SERVES 4: ABOUT 41/2 OUNCES (130 G) COOKED PORK, 1½ CUPS (233 G) VEGETABLES, AND ¼ CUP (60 ML) AU JUS PER SERVING

Nonstick cooking spray, for preparing the cooking pot

1½ teaspoons paprika

1 teaspoon poultry seasoning

1 teaspoon garlic powder

½ teaspoon black pepper

½ teaspoon salt, divided

⅛ teaspoon cayenne pepper

2 pound (908 g) boneless lean Boston butt pork roast, trimmed of fat (see Cook's Note)

1 teaspoon canola oil

2 large leeks, rinsed well, white and light green portions thinly sliced

1½ cups (360 ml) fat-free reduced-sodium chicken broth

1 pound (454 g) sweet potatoes, peeled and cut into 1-inch (2.5 cm) cubes

8 ounces (225 g) parsnips, peeled and cut into 1-inch (2.5 cm) cubes

NOTE

When purchasing pork roast, always buy at least 8 ounces (225 g) more than the recipe calls for. No matter how lean it looks . . . there's always more to trim!

Continued

In a small bowl, stir together the paprika, poultry seasoning, garlic powder, black pepper, ¼ teaspoon of salt, and the cayenne. Rub the pork all over with the paprika mixture.

On your pressure cooker, select Sauté/Browning + more to preheat the cooking pot. Once hot, coat the pot with cooking spray. Add the canola oil and tilt the pot to coat the bottom lightly. Add the pork. Cook for about 10 minutes, turning to brown on all sides. Remove the pork from the pot and set aside.

Add the leeks to the pot. Cook for 2 minutes. Add the chicken broth and bring to a boil, scraping up any browned bits from the bottom of the pot. Top with the pork.

Lock the lid in place and close the seal valve. Press the Cancel button. Press the Manual button to set the cook time for 50 minutes. When the cook time ends, use a quick pressure release.

When the valve drops, carefully remove the lid. Stir in the sweet potatoes and parsnips.

Lock the lid in place and close the seal valve. Press the Cancel button. Press the Manual button to set the cook time for 5 minutes. When the cook time ends, use a quick pressure release.

Transfer the pork to a cutting board and let rest for 15 minutes before slicing. Using a slotted spoon, remove the vegetables and place them in a bowl. Cover with aluminum foil to keep warm.

Press the Cancel button. Select Sauté/Browning + more. Bring the liquid in the cooking pot to a boil. Boil for 6 to 8 minutes, or until reduced to 1 cup (240 ml). Stir in the remaining ¼ teaspoon of salt. Serve alongside pork and vegetables.

NUTRITION FACTS

PER SERVING (423 G)

CALORIES	350	
		% DAILY VALUE
TOTAL FAT	9G	12%
SATURATED FAT	3G	15%
TRANS FAT	0G	
CHOLESTEROL	80MG	27%
SODIUM	660MG	29%
TOTAL CARBOHYDRATE	37G	13%
DIETARY FIBER	6G	21%
TOTAL SUGARS	9G	
ADDED SUGARS	0G	
PROTEIN	29G	
VITAMIN D	1MCG	6%
CALCIUM	102MG	8%
IRON	4MG	20%
POTASSIUM	1,145MG	25%

Smoky Bacon and Pork Goulash on Rice

SERVES 4: 1 CUP (100 G) MEAT MIXTURE, ½ CUP (70 G) RICE
AND ¼ CUP (60 ML) SAUCE PER SERVING

4 bacon slices, chopped

1 pound (454 g) pork shoulder blade steak, trimmed of fat and cut into 1-inch (2.5 cm) pieces

1 cup (160 g) finely chopped onions

4 ounces (115 g) sliced baby portobello mushrooms

1 can (14.5 ounces, or 410 g) stewed tomatoes

½ cup (120 ml) red wine

1 tablespoon (8 g) smoked paprika

2 teaspoons light soy sauce

2 packets (0.14 ounce, or 4 g, each) sodium-free beef bouillon granules

½ teaspoon dried oregano leaves

¼ teaspoon black pepper

¼ teaspoon salt

1 (8.8 ounces, or 250 g) pouch brown rice, such as Ben's Original Ready Rice

NOTE

The highly flavored bacon, smoked paprika, and red wine are the key ingredients here. When reduced, they create a super, SUPER rich sauce! Try it over 2 cups of cooked grits for an interesting change!

On your pressure cooker, select Sauté/Browning + more to preheat the cooking pot. Once hot, add the bacon to the pot. Cook for 5 minutes until crisp, stirring frequently. Transfer to paper towels to drain. Discard the bacon grease. Place the pork in the pot with the bacon and remaining ingredients, except the rice.

Lock the lid in place and close the seal valve. Press the Cancel button. Press the Manual button to set the cook time for 25 minutes. When the cook time ends, use a natural pressure release.

When the valve drops, carefully remove the lid.

Using a slotted spoon, transfer the meat to a bowl.

Press the Cancel button. Select Sauté/Browning + more. Bring the liquid in the pot to a boil. Cook for 10 minutes, uncovered, or until reduced to 1 cup (240 ml) of liquid.

Cook the rice according to the package directions. Serve the pork and sauce over the rice.

NUTRITION FACTS

PER SERVING (223 G)

CALORIES	250	
	% DAILY VALUE	
TOTAL FAT	6G	8%
SATURATED FAT	2G	10%
TRANS FAT	0G	
CHOLESTEROL	45MG	15%
SODIUM	650MG	28%
TOTAL CARBOHYDRATE	25G	9%
DIETARY FIBER	2G	7%
TOTAL SUGARS	5G	
ADDED SUGARS	0G	
PROTEIN	19G	
VITAMIN D	1MCG	6%
CALCIUM	38MG	2%
IRON	2MG	10%
POTASSIUM	713MG	15%

CHAPTER 4

Soups and Stews

*Soups and stews bring comfort. But the truly comforting ones usually take a long time to cook. Pressure cooking can provide that long, slow-simmered flavor and oh-so-tender texture in just minutes and without turning the veggies into mush! Choosing the right cut of meat, poultry, and vegetables plus proper timing are key elements . . . **easy elements**, though!*

Chicken and Veggie Noodle Soup

SERVES 4: 1¼ CUPS (372 G) PER SERVING

Nonstick cooking spray, for preparing the cooking pot

1 teaspoon canola oil

1 cup (160 g) chopped onion

1 cup (100 g) sliced celery

1 pound (454 g) bone-in skinless chicken thighs, trimmed of fat

1 cup (130 g) fresh or frozen sliced carrots

3 cups (720 ml) reduced-sodium chicken broth

¾ teaspoon poultry seasoning

3 ounces (85 g) no-yolk egg noodles

3 tablespoons (42 g) light butter with canola oil

½ teaspoon salt

¼ teaspoon black pepper

On your pressure cooker, select Sauté/Browning + more to preheat the cooking pot. Once hot, coat the pot with cooking spray. Add the canola oil and tilt the pot to coat the bottom lightly. Add the onion. Cook for 2 minutes. Add the celery. Cook for 1 minute. Add the chicken, carrots, chicken broth, and poultry seasoning.

Lock the lid in place and close the seal valve. Press the Cancel button. Press the Manual button to set the cook time for 15 minutes. When the cook time ends, use a natural pressure release for 5 minutes, then a quick pressure release.

When the valve drops, carefully remove the lid. Using a slotted spoon, transfer the chicken to a plate. Add the noodles to the liquid in the pot.

Lock the lid in place and close the seal valve. Press the Cancel button. Press the Manual button to set the cook time for 3 minutes. When the cook time ends, use a quick pressure release.

Remove the chicken from the bones and coarsely chop the meat. Add the chicken, butter, salt, and pepper to the noodles. Stir to combine.

NUTRITION FACTS

PER SERVING (372 G)

CALORIES	280	
	% DAILY VALUE	
TOTAL FAT	12G	15%
SATURATED FAT	3.5G	18%
TRANS FAT	0G	
CHOLESTEROL	60MG	20%
SODIUM	780MG	34%
TOTAL CARBOHYDRATE	23G	8%
DIETARY FIBER	2G	7%
TOTAL SUGARS	5G	
ADDED SUGARS	0G	
PROTEIN	20G	
VITAMIN D	0MCG	
CALCIUM	46MG	4%
IRON	2MG	10%
POTASSIUM	316MG	6%

NOTE

Be sure to use bone-in chicken thighs. They add more "calorie-free" flavor and the meat is so tender it falls off the bone!

Buffalo Wing Chicken Chili

SERVES 6: ABOUT 1 CUP (354 G) CHICKEN MIXTURE, ⅓ CUP (47 G) RICE, AND 2 TEASPOONS (5 G) BLUE CHEESE PER SERVING

Nonstick cooking spray, for coating the chicken

2 tablespoons (30 ml) extra-virgin olive oil, divided

1½ pounds (681 g) boneless skinless chicken thighs, trimmed of fat

3 cups (720 ml) reduced-sodium chicken broth

2 cans (14.5 ounces, or 410 g, each) diced fire-roasted tomatoes

8 garlic cloves, minced

3 tablespoons (45 ml) hot pepper sauce, such as Frank's, divided

1 pouch (8.8-ounce, or 250 g) brown rice, such as Uncle Ben's Ready Rice

1 ounce (28 g) crumbled reduced-fat blue cheese

On your pressure cooker, select Sauté/Browning + more to preheat the cooking pot. Once hot, add 2 teaspoons of olive oil and tilt the pot to coat the bottom lightly. Coat half the chicken with cooking spray and add it to the pot. Cook for 5 minutes *without turning*. Turn the chicken and add the uncooked chicken, chicken broth, tomatoes, garlic, and 2 tablespoons (30 ml) of hot sauce.

Lock the lid in place and close the seal valve. Press the Cancel button. Press the Manual button to set the cook time for 8 minutes. When the cook time ends, use a natural pressure release for 5 minutes, then a quick pressure release.

When the valve drops, carefully remove the lid. Using a fork, stir the chili to break up the chicken in the pot. Stir in the remaining 1 tablespoon plus 1 teaspoon (20 ml) of olive oil and 1 tablespoon (15 ml) of hot sauce.

Prepare the rice according to the package directions and divide it among 6 bowls. Top with equal amounts of the chili and sprinkle evenly with the blue cheese.

NUTRITION FACTS

PER SERVING (410 G)

CALORIES	340	
	% DAILY VALUE	
TOTAL FAT	15G	19%
SATURATED FAT	4G	20%
TRANS FAT	0G	
CHOLESTEROL	80MG	27%
SODIUM	790MG	34%
TOTAL CARBOHYDRATE	20G	7%
DIETARY FIBER	2G	7%
TOTAL SUGARS	5G	
ADDED SUGARS	0G	
PROTEIN	27G	
VITAMIN D	0MCG	
CALCIUM	87MG	6%
IRON	3MG	15%
POTASSIUM	311MG	6%

Italian Sausage and Veggie Soup Stew

SERVES 4: 1½ CUPS (332 G) PER SERVING

Nonstick cooking spray, for preparing the cooking pot

3 hot Italian turkey sausage links (3 ounces, or 85 g, each), casings removed

1 cup (100 g) fresh or (124 g) frozen cut green beans

1 cup (130 g) fresh or frozen sliced carrots

1 package (8 ounces, or 225 g) sliced mushrooms

1 can (14.5 ounces, or 410 g) diced fire-roasted tomatoes with garlic

1 cup (240 ml) water

¼ teaspoon dried fennel or Italian seasoning

1 medium zucchini, chopped

1 ounce (28 g) Asiago cheese, shredded

On your pressure cooker, select Sauté/Browning + more to preheat the cooking pot. Once hot, coat the pot with cooking spray. Add the sausage. Cook for 4 minutes, stirring frequently. Add the green beans, carrots, mushrooms, tomatoes, water, and fennel.

Lock the lid in place and close the seal valve. Press the Cancel button. Press the Manual button to set the cook time for 15 minutes. When the cook time ends, use a quick pressure release.

When the valve drops, carefully remove the lid. Stir in the zucchini. Press the Cancel button. Select Sauté/Browning + more. Bring the soup stew to a boil. Cook, uncovered, for 3 minutes, or until the zucchini is just crisp-tender.

Top with the cheese before serving.

NOTE

For a thinner consistency, add ½ cup (120 ml) water at the end of the cook time.

NUTRITION FACTS

PER SERVING (332 G)

CALORIES	200	
	% DAILY VALUE	
TOTAL FAT	10G	13%
SATURATED FAT	1.5G	8%
TRANS FAT	0G	
CHOLESTEROL	45MG	15%
SODIUM	700MG	30%
TOTAL CARBOHYDRATE	13G	5%
DIETARY FIBER	5G	18%
TOTAL SUGARS	7G	
ADDED SUGARS	0G	
PROTEIN	16G	
VITAMIN D	0MCG	
CALCIUM	120MG	10%
IRON	3MG	15%
POTASSIUM	710MG	15%

Beef and Pinto Bean Chili Stew

SERVES 4: 1¼ CUPS (332 G) PER SERVING

Nonstick cooking spray, for preparing the cooking pot

12 ounces (340 g) lean ground beef

4 ounces (115 g) dried pinto beans, rinsed and drained

12 ounces (360 ml) light beer (such as Miller Lite)

1 (10-ounce, or 280 g) can diced tomatoes with lime juice and cilantro

1 (4.5-ounce, or 130 g) can chopped mild green chiles

¾ cup (123.75 g) frozen corn

1 cup (240 ml) water

1 (1-ounce, or 28 g) package 30% reduced-sodium taco seasoning

½ cup chopped fresh cilantro (8 g) or chopped scallion (50 g)

On your pressure cooker, select Sauté/Browning + more to preheat the cooking pot. Once hot, coat the pot with cooking spray. Add the ground beef. Cook for about 3 minutes until browned, stirring frequently. Add the beans, beer, tomatoes, chiles, corn, and water.

Lock the lid in place and close the seal valve. Press the Cancel button. Press the Manual button to set the cook time for 35 minutes. When the cook time ends, use a quick pressure release.

When the valve drops, carefully remove the lid. Stir in the taco seasoning and cilantro (or scallion). Let stand, uncovered, for 10 minutes to absorb the flavors.

NUTRITION FACTS

SERVING SIZE (332 G)		
CALORIES	310	
	% DAILY VALUE	
TOTAL FAT	6G	8%
SATURATED FAT	3G	15%
TRANS FAT	0G	
CHOLESTEROL	55MG	18%
SODIUM	810MG	35%
TOTAL CARBOHYDRATE	34G	12%
DIETARY FIBER	8G	29%
TOTAL SUGARS	6G	
ADDED SUGARS	0G	
PROTEIN	25G	
VITAMIN D	0MCG	
CALCIUM	63MG	4%
IRON	3MG	15%
POTASSIUM	473MG	10%

Hearty Corn, Potato, and Onion Chowder with Shrimp

SERVES 4: 1¼ CUPS (355 G) PER SERVING

1 tablespoon (15 ml) canola oil

2 cups (320 g) chopped onion

¾ cup (180 ml) water

8 ounces (225 g) petite Yukon gold potatoes, cut into 1-inch (2.5 cm) chunks

¾ cup (124 g) frozen corn

⅛ teaspoon red pepper flakes (optional)

12 ounces (340 g) fresh or frozen shrimp, peeled and deveined

2 teaspoons seafood seasoning, such as Old Bay

½ cup (120 ml) 2% milk

⅓ cup (43 g) frozen green peas

2 tablespoons (28 g) light butter with canola oil

¼ teaspoon salt

¼ teaspoon black pepper, or to taste

¼ cup (25 g) chopped scallion

NOTE

Little yellow Yukon gold potatoes are sold in mesh bags in the produce section of major supermarkets, but if they're not available, use the larger version cut into 1-inch (2.5 cm) chunks. Red potatoes may be substituted, but the yellow potatoes add a buttery look to the dish.

On your pressure cooker, select Sauté/Browning + more to preheat the cooking pot. Once hot, add the canola oil and tilt the pot to coat the bottom lightly. Add the onion. Cook for 4 minutes, or until beginning to turn golden (do not let them become richly browned), stirring frequently. Add the water, potatoes, corn, and red pepper flakes (if using).

Lock the lid in place and close the seal valve. Press the Cancel button. Press the Manual button to set the cook time for 5 minutes. When the cook time ends, use a quick pressure release.

When the valve drops, carefully remove the lid. Press the Cancel button. Select Sauté/Browning + more. Bring the chowder to a boil. Add the shrimp and seafood seasoning. Return the mixture to a boil and cook for 4 minutes, stirring occasionally. Turn off the pressure cooker. Stir in the milk, peas, butter, salt, and pepper. Let stand for 5 minutes to absorb the flavors. Serve topped with the scallions.

NUTRITION FACTS

PER SERVING (355 G)

CALORIES	230	
	% DAILY VALUE	
TOTAL FAT	8G	10%
SATURATED FAT	2G	10%
TRANS FAT	0G	
CHOLESTEROL	110MG	37%
SODIUM	660MG	29%
TOTAL CARBOHYDRATE	24G	9%
DIETARY FIBER	3G	11%
TOTAL SUGARS	6G	
ADDED SUGARS	0G	
PROTEIN	15G	
VITAMIN D	0MCG	
CALCIUM	108MG	8%
IRON	1MG	6%
POTASSIUM	472MG	10%

Seafood and Veggie Gumbo Stew

SERVES 12: 1 CUP (233 G) GUMBO PLUS ⅓ CUP (67 G) RICE PER SERVING

3 tablespoons (23 g) all-purpose flour

¼ cup (60 ml) canola oil

1½ cups (150 g) chopped celery

3 cups (273 g) frozen pepper stir-fry

2 cans (14.5 ounces, or 410 g, each) stewed tomatoes

2 cups (480 ml) water

1½ tablespoons (11 g) seafood seasoning, such as Old Bay, divided

4 bay leaves

1 teaspoon garlic powder

12 ounces (340 g) frozen tilapia fillets

12 ounces (340 g) frozen peeled, deveined medium shrimp

1 pound (454 g) frozen cut okra

1 tablespoon (15 ml) hot sauce, such as Franks

1 teaspoon salt

4 cups (800 g) cooked brown rice or (740 g) cooked white rice

NOTE

This is even better the next day and leftovers freeze well for up to two months; freeze the gumbo and rice separately. However, it's best to freeze in individual servings, if possible, for easy thawing and portion control. May thaw in the refrigerator overnight then reheat in a covered saucepan over low heat. Timing will vary depending on how much is frozen.

Continued

On your pressure cooker, select Sauté/Browning + more to preheat the cooking pot. Once hot, combine the flour and canola oil in the pot. Cook for 10 minutes, stirring constantly with a flat spatula until light brown.

Add the celery. Cook for 3 minutes, stirring frequently. Stir in the frozen pepper stir-fry, tomatoes, water, 1 tablespoon (7 g) of seafood seasoning, the bay leaves, and garlic powder.

Lock the lid in place and close the seal valve. Press the Cancel button. Press the Manual button to set the cook time for 20 minutes. When the cook time ends, use a natural pressure release.

When the valve drops, carefully remove the lid. Add the tilapia, shrimp, okra, hot sauce, salt, and remaining seafood seasoning.

Lock the lid in place and close the seal valve. Press the Cancel button. Press the Manual button to set the cook time for 2 minutes. When the cook time ends, use a quick pressure release.

When the valve drops, carefully remove the lid. Stir and let stand, uncovered, for 15 minutes to thicken and allow the flavors to develop. (Note: The ingredients will continue to cook while standing.) Serve over the rice.

NUTRITION FACTS

PER SERVING (233 G)

CALORIES	220	
		% DAILY VALUE
TOTAL FAT	6G	8%
SATURATED FAT	0.5G	3%
TRANS FAT	0G	
CHOLESTEROL	50MG	17%
SODIUM	690MG	30%
TOTAL CARBOHYDRATE	28G	10%
DIETARY FIBER	3G	11%
TOTAL SUGARS	4G	
ADDED SUGARS	0G	
PROTEIN	13G	
VITAMIN D	1MCG	6%
CALCIUM	82MG	6%
IRON	2MG	10%
POTASSIUM	435MG	10%

Freezer-to-Pot Broccoli, Corn, and Pepper Soup

SERVES 4: 1½ CUPS (514 G) PER SERVING

4 cups (624 g) frozen broccoli florets

3 cups (315 g) frozen peppers and onions

2 cups (364 g) frozen mixed vegetables

½ cup (120 ml) water

½ teaspoon dried thyme

1 bay leaf

⅛ teaspoon red pepper flakes

2 cups (480 ml) 2% milk, divided

1 tablespoon (8 g) cornstarch

½ teaspoon salt

¼ teaspoon black pepper

3 ounces (85 g) shredded reduced-fat sharp Cheddar cheese

1½ ounces (43 g) crumbled reduced-fat blue cheese

¼ cup (15 g) chopped fresh parsley

In the pressure cooker cooking pot, combine the frozen broccoli, peppers and onions, mixed vegetables, water, thyme, bay leaf, and red pepper flakes.

Lock the lid in place and close the seal valve. Press the Manual button to set the cook time for 3 minutes. When the cook time ends, use a quick pressure release.

When the valve drops, carefully remove the lid. Press the Cancel button. Select Sauté/Browning + more. In a small bowl, whisk ¼ cup (60 ml) of milk and the cornstarch until the cornstarch dissolves. Stir this slurry into the broccoli mixture along with ¾ cup (180 ml) of milk. Bring to a boil. Boil for 1 minute, stirring constantly.

Turn off the pressure cooker. Stir in remaining 1 cup (240 ml) of milk, the salt, and pepper. Gradually stir in the cheeses. Serve topped with the parsley.

NUTRITION FACTS

PER SERVING (514 G)

CALORIES	270	
	% DAILY VALUE	
TOTAL FAT	9G	12%
SATURATED FAT	6G	30%
TRANS FAT	0G	
CHOLESTEROL	30MG	10%
SODIUM	690MG	30%
TOTAL CARBOHYDRATE	27G	10%
DIETARY FIBER	6G	21%
TOTAL SUGARS	13G	
ADDED SUGARS	0G	
PROTEIN	17G	
VITAMIN D	2MCG	10%
CALCIUM	426MG	35%
IRON	1MG	6%
POTASSIUM	338MG	8%

Cattle Trail Chili

SERVES 7: ABOUT 1 CUP (308 G) PER SERVING

1 tablespoon (15 ml) canola oil

1 pound (454 g) 93% fat-free ground turkey

1½ cups (240 g) chopped onion

1 can (14.5 ounces, or 410 g) stewed tomatoes

2 tablespoons (32 g) tomato paste

1 can (15 ounces, or 425 g) no-salt-added dark red kidney beans, drained and rinsed

12 ounces (360 ml) light beer, such as Miller Lite

3 tablespoons (23 g) chili powder

1½ tablespoons (11 g) ground cumin

2 teaspoons dried oregano leaves

1 teaspoon garlic powder

1 tablespoon (20 g) honey

½ teaspoon salt

½ cup (8 g) chopped fresh cilantro or (30 g) parsley

On your pressure cooker, select Sauté/Browning + more to preheat the cooking pot. Once hot, add the canola oil and tilt the pot to coat the bottom lightly. Add the ground turkey. Cook for 4 minutes, or until browned, stirring occasionally. Add the onion, tomatoes, tomato paste, kidney beans, beer, chili powder, cumin, oregano, and garlic powder.

Lock the lid in place and close the seal valve. Press the Cancel button. Press the Manual button to set the cook time for 15 minutes. When the cook time ends, use a quick pressure release.

When the valve drops, carefully remove the lid. Stir in the honey and salt. Serve garnished with the cilantro.

NUTRITION FACTS

PER SERVING (308 G)		
CALORIES	260	
	% DAILY VALUE	
TOTAL FAT	10G	13%
SATURATED FAT	2G	10%
TRANS FAT	0G	
CHOLESTEROL	55MG	18%
SODIUM	570MG	25%
TOTAL CARBOHYDRATE	22G	8%
DIETARY FIBER	7G	25%
TOTAL SUGARS	7G	
ADDED SUGARS	3G	6%
PROTEIN	19G	
VITAMIN D	0MCG	
CALCIUM	89MG	6%
IRON	3MG	15%
POTASSIUM	526MG	10%

Vegetable Beef Soup

SERVES 6: ABOUT 1⅓ CUPS (321 G) PER SERVING

2 tablespoons (30 ml) extra-virgin olive oil, divided

1½ pounds (679 g) boneless lean beef chuck, trimmed of fat and cut into 1-inch (2.5 cm) cubes

1 package (14 ounces, or 395 g) frozen pepper stir-fry

2 cups (200 g) fresh or (248 g) frozen green beans, cut into 2-inch (5 cm) pieces

1 cup (130 g) fresh or frozen sliced carrots

1 can (14.5 ounces, or 410 g) stewed tomatoes

1 cup (240 ml) water

3 packets (0.14 ounce, or 4 g, each) sodium-free beef bouillon granules

1 tablespoon (3 g) dried oregano leaves

4 cups (360 g) coarsely chopped green cabbage

3 tablespoons (45 g) ketchup

1 tablespoon (15 ml) Worcestershire sauce

1 teaspoon salt

NOTE

It's best to freeze in individual servings, if possible, for easy thawing and portion control. May thaw in the refrigerator overnight then reheat in a covered saucepan over low heat. Timing will vary depending on how much is frozen.

Continued

On your pressure cooker, select Sauté/Browning + more to preheat the cooking pot. Once hot, add 1 tablespoon (15 ml) of olive oil and tilt the pot to coat the bottom lightly. Add half the beef. Cook for 5 minutes *without stirring*. Stir in the remaining beef and top it with the frozen pepper stir-fry, green beans, carrots, tomatoes, water, bouillon granules, and oregano.

Lock the lid in place and close the seal valve. Press the Cancel button. Press the Manual button to set the cook time for 20 minutes. When the cook time ends, use a quick pressure release.

When the valve drops, carefully remove the lid. Add the cabbage, ketchup, Worcestershire sauce, salt, and remaining 1 tablespoon (15 ml) of olive oil.

Lock the lid in place and close the seal valve. Press the Cancel button. Press the Manual button to set the cook time for 4 minutes. When the cook time ends, use a natural pressure release for 15 minutes, then a quick pressure release.

When the valve drops, carefully remove the lid and serve.

NUTRITION FACTS

PER SERVING (321 G)

CALORIES	250	
		% DAILY VALUE
TOTAL FAT	9G	12%
SATURATED FAT	2.5G	13%
TRANS FAT	0G	
CHOLESTEROL	45MG	15%
SODIUM	720MG	31%
TOTAL CARBOHYDRATE	16G	6%
DIETARY FIBER	4G	14%
TOTAL SUGARS	10G	
ADDED SUGARS	2G	4%
PROTEIN	24G	
VITAMIN D	0MCG	
CALCIUM	69MG	6%
IRON	3MG	15%
POTASSIUM	335MG	8%

Coconut Curry Pork Bowls

SERVES 4: 1 CUP (308 G) PORK MIXTURE PLUS ABOUT
½ CUP (63 G) RICE PER SERVING

2 cups (182 g) frozen pepper stir-fry

1 can (8 ounces, or 225 g) pineapple tidbits in juice, drained

⅓ cup (50 g) raisins

1 cup (240 ml) reduced-sodium chicken broth, divided

1½ tablespoons (9 g) curry powder

1 teaspoon garlic powder

2 bone-in pork sirloin chops (6 ounces, or 170 g, each), trimmed of fat

2 teaspoons roasted red chili paste

1 cup (240 ml) light coconut milk

½ cup (65 g) frozen green peas

2 teaspoons grated peeled fresh ginger

½ teaspoon salt

¼ cup (4 g) chopped fresh cilantro leaves

1 pouch (8.8 ounce, or 250 g) brown rice, such as Ben's Original Ready Rice

NOTE

This is definitely the perfect way to debone effortlessly. The pork literally falls off the bones while cooking so all you have to do is remove them from the pot and give everything a quick stir to break down the larger pieces.

Continued

In your pressure cooker cooking pot, combine the frozen pepper stir-fry, pineapple, raisins, ¾ cup (180 ml) of chicken broth, the curry powder, and garlic powder. Top with the pork chops. In a small bowl, stir together the remaining ¼ cup (60 ml) of broth and the chili paste. Spoon this over the pork.

Lock the lid in place and close the seal valve. Press the Manual button to set the cook time for 18 minutes. When the cook time ends, use a quick pressure release.

When the valve drops, carefully remove the lid. Remove the bones from the pot. Stir in the coconut milk, peas, ginger, salt, and cilantro. (Note: Stirring the mixture will help break the pork into smaller pieces.)

Prepare the rice according to the package directions. Spoon equal amounts of the rice into 4 bowls and spoon the pork curry mixture on top.

NUTRITION FACTS

PER SERVING (371 G)		
CALORIES	330	
		% DAILY VALUE
TOTAL FAT	8G	10%
SATURATED FAT	5G	25%
TRANS FAT	0G	
CHOLESTEROL	40MG	13%
SODIUM	550MG	24%
TOTAL CARBOHYDRATE	45G	16%
DIETARY FIBER	2G	7%
TOTAL SUGARS	15G	
ADDED SUGARS	0G	
PROTEIN	18G	
VITAMIN D	0MCG	
CALCIUM	24MG	2%
IRON	1MG	6%
POTASSIUM	469MG	10%

CHAPTER 5

Protein and Vegetable Combination Dinners

There has been a great deal of emphasis on recipes to incorporate a variety of green, yellow, and red vegetables into more and more dishes. This emphasis helps to keep the calorie count low while providing generous serving sizes. Some are served in layers while others are tossed together. Variety, color, and texture all play important nutritional roles adding interest and character, too. Try using vegetables as a base instead of the higher-calorie, higher-carb ingredients, such as pasta and rice for a change. You'll be surprised how the new flavor combinations will satisfy and your meals will become even more interesting!

Picante Chicken on Yellow Squash

SERVES 4: ¾ CUP (102 G) SQUASH, 3 OUNCES (85 G) COOKED CHICKEN,
AND ¼ CUP (60 ML) SAUCE PER SERVING

Nonstick cooking spray, for preparing the cooking pot

12 ounces (340 g) yellow crookneck squash, thinly sliced

⅓ cup (53 g) chopped onion

¼ teaspoon black pepper

½ cup (120 ml) water

4 boneless skinless chicken thighs (about 1 pound, or 454 g, total), trimmed of fat

1 cup (240 ml) picante sauce

1 teaspoon smoked paprika

½ teaspoon sugar

On your pressure cooker, select Sauté/Browning + more to preheat the cooking pot. Once hot, coat the pot with cooking spray. Add the squash, onion, and pepper. Cook for 5 minutes, or until just crisp-tender and beginning to lightly brown, stirring frequently. Transfer the mixture to a plate and cover with aluminum foil to keep warm.

Add the water to the cooking pot, scraping up any browned bits from the bottom of the pot. Add the chicken, picante sauce, and paprika.

Lock the lid in place and close the seal valve. Press the Cancel button. Press the Manual button to set the cook time for 8 minutes. When the cook time ends, use a quick pressure release.

When the valve drops, carefully remove the lid. Using a slotted spoon, remove the chicken and place it on the squash mixture. Re-cover and set aside.

Press the Cancel button. Select Sauté/Browning + more. Stir the sugar into the sauce and bring it to a boil. Boil for 5 minutes, or until reduced to 1 cup (240 ml) of liquid. Spoon the sauce over the chicken and squash.

NUTRITION FACTS

PER SERVING (247 G)		
CALORIES	200	
	% DAILY VALUE	
TOTAL FAT	8G	10%
SATURATED FAT	2.5G	13%
TRANS FAT	0G	
CHOLESTEROL	75MG	2%
SODIUM	570MG	25%
TOTAL CARBOHYDRATE	9G	3%
DIETARY FIBER	2G	7%
TOTAL SUGARS	6G	
ADDED SUGARS	1G	2%
PROTEIN	22G	
VITAMIN D	0MCG	
CALCIUM	30MG	2%
IRON	2MG	10%
POTASSIUM	362MG	8%

NOTE

Who needs rice?! Lightly browning the squash and onion creates a rich and colorful base for this smoky enchilada-tasting dish.

Greek Lemon Chicken with Asparagus

SERVES 4: 2 CHICKEN THIGHS AND ABOUT 1 CUP (105 G) ASPARAGUS PER SERVING

2 teaspoons salt-free grilling blend

1 teaspoon paprika

8 bone-in skinless chicken thighs (about 2¼ pounds, or 1 kg, total)

½ cup (120 ml) dry white wine

½ cup (120 ml) water

2 teaspoons grated lemon zest

2 tablespoons (30 ml) fresh lemon juice

1 tablespoon (15 ml) extra-virgin olive oil

1 garlic clove, minced

2 teaspoons dried dill

½ teaspoon dried oregano leaves

½ teaspoon salt

1 pound (454 g) fresh or frozen cut asparagus

In a small bowl, stir together the seasoning blend and paprika. Sprinkle the spices evenly over the smooth side of the chicken. Pour the white wine and water into the pressure cooker cooking pot. Top with the chicken pieces, overlapping them slightly.

Lock the lid in place and close the seal valve. Press the Manual button to set the cook time for 20 minutes. When the cook time ends, use a natural pressure release for 10 minutes, then a quick pressure release.

When the valve drops, carefully remove the lid. Using a slotted spoon, remove the chicken and place it smooth-side up on a rimmed platter or in a shallow pasta bowl.

In a small bowl, whisk the lemon zest, lemon juice, olive oil, and garlic. Drizzle this all over the chicken. Sprinkle it evenly with the dill, oregano, and salt. Cover with aluminum foil and let rest for 10 minutes to absorb the flavors.

Meanwhile, press the Cancel button on the cooker. Select Sauté/Browning + more. Bring the liquid in the pot to a boil. Add the asparagus. Return the mixture to a boil and cook for 2 to 3 minutes, or until crisp-tender. Remove with a slotted spoon and arrange around the chicken.

NUTRITION FACTS

PER SERVING (267 G)

CALORIES	330	
		% DAILY VALUE
TOTAL FAT	14G	18%
SATURATED FAT	3.5G	18%
TRANS FAT	0G	
CHOLESTEROL	175MG	58%
SODIUM	620MG	27%
TOTAL CARBOHYDRATE	13G	5%
DIETARY FIBER	4G	14%
TOTAL SUGARS	4G	
ADDED SUGARS	0G	
PROTEIN	37G	
VITAMIN D	0MCG	
CALCIUM	44MG	4%
IRON	4MG	20%
POTASSIUM	549MG	10%

Salmon with Spinach and Horseradish Sour Cream

SERVES 4: ABOUT 4 OUNCES (115 G) COOKED SALMON,
¾ CUP (135 G) SPINACH, AND 2 TABLESPOONS (32.5 G) SAUCE PER SERVING

½ cup (115 g) light sour cream

1 tablespoon (15 g) prepared horseradish

¾ teaspoon salt, divided

Nonstick cooking spray, for preparing the cooking pot

1 teaspoon canola oil

2 (9-ounce, or 255 g) package fresh spinach

2 tablespoons (28 g) light butter with canola oil

2 lemons

¾ cup (180 ml) water

4 (6-ounce, or 170 g) frozen salmon fillets

¼ teaspoon black pepper

½ teaspoon dried thyme

In a small bowl, stir together the sour cream, horseradish, and ¼ teaspoon salt. Set aside.

On your pressure cooker, select Sauté/Browning + more to preheat the cooking pot. Once hot, coat the cooking pot with cooking spray. Add the canola oil and tilt the pot to coat the bottom lightly. Add half the spinach. Cook for 2 minutes, or until just beginning to wilt slightly, stirring frequently. Transfer to a dinner or serving plate and set aside.

Coat the cooking pot again with cooking spray. Add the remaining spinach and cook until just wilted. Transfer to the plate with the other spinach. Using the back of a spoon, spread the butter over the spinach and sprinkle with ¼ teaspoon of salt. Do not stir. Cover to keep warm.

Slice 1 lemon and place it into the cooking pot. Put a steamer basket into the pot and pour in the water. Place the frozen salmon in the basket. Sprinkle with the remaining ¼ teaspoon of salt, the pepper, and the thyme.

Lock the lid in place and close the seal valve. Press the Cancel button. Press the Manual button to set the cook time for 4 minutes. When the cook time ends, use a quick pressure release.

When the valve drops, carefully remove the lid. Remove the salmon and place it over the spinach. Squeeze the juice of the remaining lemon over the salmon and top with the sour cream mixture.

NUTRITION FACTS

SERVING SIZE (297 G)		
CALORIES	260	
	% DAILY VALUE	
TOTAL FAT	12G	15%
SATURATED FAT	4G	20%
TRANS FAT	0G	
CHOLESTEROL	75MG	25%
SODIUM	690MG	30%
TOTAL CARBOHYDRATE	7G	3%
DIETARY FIBER	3G	11%
TOTAL SUGARS	0G	
ADDED SUGARS	0G	
PROTEIN	28G	
VITAMIN D	0MCG	
CALCIUM	190MG	15%
IRON	5MG	30%
POTASSIUM	72MG	2%

Tender Pork Chops in Rich Onion Sauce

SERVES 4: ABOUT 5 OUNCES (140 G) COOKED PORK AND ¼ CUP (25 G)
ONION MIXTURE PER SERVING

Nonstick cooking spray, for preparing the cooking pot

1 teaspoon canola oil

2 cups (320 g) thinly sliced onions

1 cup (240 ml) water

1 teaspoon balsamic vinegar

4 bone-in pork loin chops (8 ounces, or 225 g, each), about 1-inch (2.5 cm) thick, trimmed of fat

2 teaspoons sodium-free beef bouillon granulates

¾ teaspoon black pepper

½ teaspoon paprika

½ teaspoon garlic powder

½ teaspoon salt, divided

¼ teaspoon sugar

On your pressure cooker, select Sauté/Browning + more to preheat the cooking pot. Once hot, coat the pot with cooking spray. Add the canola oil and tilt the pot to coat the bottom lightly. Add the onions. Cook for 10 minutes, stirring occasionally. Stir in the water and vinegar. Place the pork chops on top. Sprinkle with the bouillon granules, pepper, paprika, garlic powder, and ¼ teaspoon of salt.

Lock the lid in place and close the seal valve. Press the Cancel button. Press the Manual button to set the cook time for 18 minutes. When the cook time ends, use a natural pressure release for 10 minutes, then a quick pressure release.

When the valve drops, carefully remove the lid. Add the remaining ¼ teaspoon of salt and the sugar to the mixture in the pot. Stir, making sure the pork chops are covered with the onion mixture.

Press the Cancel button. Select Sauté/Browning + more. Bring the mixture to a boil. Cook for 10 minutes, or until the onion mixture is slightly thickened and reduced to 1 cup (100 g).

NUTRITION FACTS

PER SERVING (165 G)		
CALORIES	240	
		% DAILY VALUE
TOTAL FAT	7G	9%
SATURATED FAT	2G	10%
TRANS FAT	0G	
CHOLESTEROL	110MG	37%
SODIUM	380MG	17%
TOTAL CARBOHYDRATE	8G	3%
DIETARY FIBER	1G	4%
TOTAL SUGARS	4G	
ADDED SUGARS	0G	
PROTEIN	35G	
VITAMIN D	1MCG	6%
CALCIUM	47MG	4%
IRON	1MG	6%
POTASSIUM	683MG	15%

Italian Sausage–Stuffed Peppers

SERVES 4: 1 STUFFED PEPPER PER SERVING

12 ounces (340 g) ground Italian turkey sausage

4 large bell peppers, any color; tops cut off, chopped, and reserved; seeded

¼ cup (20 g) oats, any variety

¾ cup (184 g) no-salt-added tomato sauce, divided

1 large egg

⅛ teaspoon red pepper flakes

1 cup (240 ml) water

1 ounce (28 g) shredded part-skim mozzarella cheese

2 tablespoons (12.5 g) grated Parmesan cheese

In a medium bowl, mix together the turkey sausage, chopped pepper tops, oats, ¼ cup (61 g) of tomato sauce, the egg, and red pepper flakes. Divide the turkey mixture into 4 portions, and stuff each pepper with 1 portion.

Place the water in the cooking pot and set a trivet in the pot. Arrange the stuffed peppers on the trivet. Top each pepper with 2 tablespoons of the remaining tomato sauce.

Lock the lid in place and close the seal valve. Press the Manual button to set the cook time for 15 minutes. When the cook time ends, use a natural pressure release.

When the valve drops, carefully remove the lid. Top the peppers with equal amounts of the mozzarella and Parmesan cheeses.

NUTRITION FACTS

PER SERVING (325 G)

CALORIES	280	
	% DAILY VALUE	
TOTAL FAT	14G	18%
SATURATED FAT	2G	10%
TRANS FAT	0G	
CHOLESTEROL	105MG	35%
SODIUM	700MG	30%
TOTAL CARBOHYDRATE	17G	6%
DIETARY FIBER	4G	14%
TOTAL SUGARS	8G	
ADDED SUGARS	0G	
PROTEIN	22G	
VITAMIN D	0MCG	
CALCIUM	119MG	10%
IRON	3MG	15%
POTASSIUM	343MG	8%

NOTE

When purchasing bell peppers, choose the wider, fatter variety rather than the narrower ones. They're easier to fill and keep their balance while cooking.

Chicken Cacciatore on Butternut Squash Spirals

SERVES 4: 1 THIGH, ¾ CUP (180 ML) TOMATO MIXTURE, AND ¾ CUP (160 G) SPIRALS PER SERVING

Nonstick cooking spray, for preparing the cooking pot

1½ cups (240 g) chopped onion

1 large green bell pepper, thinly sliced

1 (8-ounce, or 225 g) package sliced mushrooms

1 cup (149 g) grape tomatoes

½ cup (120 ml) dry white wine

1½ tablespoons (23 ml) Worcestershire sauce

1 teaspoon dried oregano

4 bone-in chicken thighs, skin removed (1½ pounds, or 681 g, after removing the skin)

¾ teaspoon salt

2 tablespoons (32 g) tomato paste

1 teaspoon sugar

1 (12-ounce, or 340 g) package frozen butternut squash veggie spirals

On your pressure cooker, select Sauté/Browning + more to preheat the cooking pot. Once hot, coat the pot with cooking spray. Add the onion. Cook for 3 minutes, or until beginning to lightly brown, stirring occasionally. Stir in the green bell pepper, mushrooms, tomatoes, wine, Worcestershire, and oregano. Place the chicken on top, smooth side down, and sprinkle with salt.

Lock the lid in place and close the seal valve. Press the Cancel button. Press the Manual button to set the cook time for 10 minutes. When the cook time ends, use a natural pressure release.

When the valve drops, carefully remove the lid. Using a slotted spoon, transfer the chicken to a rimmed platter or shallow pasta bowl, smooth side up.

Press the Cancel button. Select Sauté/Browning + more. Using a fork, stir in the tomato paste and sugar, breaking up the tomatoes while stirring. Cook, uncovered, for 10 minutes, or until thickened and reduced to 3 cups (720 ml).

Meanwhile, cook the squash in the microwave according to the package directions. Place the squash around the chicken and spoon the vegetable mixture over all.

NUTRITION FACTS

PER SERVING (394 G)

CALORIES	310	
	% DAILY VALUE	
TOTAL FAT	10G	13%
SATURATED FAT	2.5G	13%
TRANS FAT	0G	
CHOLESTEROL	85MG	28%
SODIUM	640MG	28%
TOTAL CARBOHYDRATE	27G	10%
DIETARY FIBER	4G	14%
TOTAL SUGARS	11G	
ADDED SUGARS	1G	2%
PROTEIN	29G	
VITAMIN D	0MCG	
CALCIUM	77MG	6%
IRON	3MG	15%
POTASSIUM	992MG	20%

Italian Meatballs and Simple Sauce on Zucchini Noodles

SERVES 4: 8 MEATBALLS, ABOUT ½ CUP (125 ML) SAUCE, AND ABOUT 3/4 CUP (85 G) ZUCCHINI PER SERVING

Nonstick cooking spray, for preparing the cooking pot

12 ounces (340 g) 93% lean ground turkey

3.5-ounce (100 g) Italian turkey sausage link, casing removed

⅔ cup (33 g) panko bread crumbs

½ cup (30 g) finely chopped fresh parsley

2 large eggs, beaten

2 teaspoons dried basil

1 teaspoon dried rosemary

½ teaspoon dried fennel

¼ teaspoon red pepper flakes

2 cups (500 g) prepared lower-sodium spaghetti sauce, such as Prego Heart Smart

½ cup (120 ml) red wine

2 teaspoons honey

1 package (12 ounces, or 340 g) frozen zucchini spirals

4 teaspoons (8 g) grated Parmesan cheese

NOTE

When buying prepared spaghetti sauce, look for those that contain the lowest sodium. You have more control over your sodium intake that way . . . even if you need to add a bit more salt to the final dish.

In a medium bowl, mix together the ground turkey, sausage, bread crumbs, parsley, beaten eggs, basil, rosemary, fennel, and red pepper flakes. Shape the mixture into about 32 small (1-inch, or 2.5 cm) balls.

On your pressure cooker, select Sauté/Browning + more to preheat the cooking pot. Once hot, coat the pot with cooking spray. Add the meatballs to the pot in a single layer. (Note: It will be snug.) Cook for 3 minutes *without turning*.

In the medium bowl, stir together the spaghetti sauce and red wine. Pour the sauce evenly over the meatballs. *Do not stir.*

Lock the lid in place and close the seal valve. Press the Cancel button. Press the Manual button to set the cook time for 4 minutes. When the cook time ends, use a quick pressure release.

When the valve drops, carefully remove the lid. Drizzle the honey over all and gently toss to combine.

Meanwhile, cook the zucchini according to the package directions. Serve the meatballs and sauce over the zucchini and sprinkle with the Parmesan.

NUTRITION FACTS

PER SERVING (402 G)

CALORIES	330	
		% DAILY VALUE
TOTAL FAT	9G	12%
SATURATED FAT	1.5G	8%
TRANS FAT	0G	
CHOLESTEROL	145MG	48%
SODIUM	680MG	30%
TOTAL CARBOHYDRATE	27G	10%
DIETARY FIBER	1G	4%
TOTAL SUGARS	15G	
ADDED SUGARS	3G	6%
PROTEIN	34G	
VITAMIN D	1MCG	6%
CALCIUM	123MG	10%
IRON	4MG	20%
POTASSIUM	717MG	15%

Flank Strips with Sweet Balsamic Glaze on Arugula

SERVES 4: 3 OUNCES (85 G) COOKED BEEF AND 1 CUP (20 G) ARUGULA PER SERVING

1¼ pounds (568 g) flank steak, cut across the grain into thin strips

1 cup (240 ml) light beer

8 garlic cloves

2 tablespoons (30 ml) balsamic vinegar

2 tablespoons (30 ml) light soy sauce

1 tablespoon (15 ml) Worcestershire sauce

1 tablespoon (12.5 g) sugar

¼ teaspoon salt

Pinch of cayenne pepper

4 cups (80 g) arugula

In your pressure cooker cooking pot, combine the beef, beer, and garlic.

Lock the lid in place and close the seal valve. Press the Manual button to set the cook time to 10 minutes. When the cook time ends, use a natural pressure release.

When the valve drops, carefully remove the lid. Remove the beef and garlic and set aside. Reserve ¼ cup (60 ml) of the cooking liquid and discard the rest.

Press the Cancel button. Select Sauté/Browning + more. Return the reserved ¼ cup (60 ml) of cooking liquid to the pot and add the vinegar, soy sauce, Worcestershire sauce, sugar, salt, and cayenne. Bring the mixture to a boil. Boil for 3 minutes.

Return the beef and garlic to the pot. Cook for 2 minutes, or until glazed and the liquid has evaporated, stirring frequently. Serve the beef over the arugula.

NUTRITION FACTS

PER SERVING (105 G)		
CALORIES	240	
		% DAILY VALUE
TOTAL FAT	8G	10%
SATURATED FAT	3G	15%
TRANS FAT	0G	
CHOLESTEROL	90MG	30%
SODIUM	570MG	25%
TOTAL CARBOHYDRATE	8G	3%
DIETARY FIBER	0G	
TOTAL SUGARS	5G	
ADDED SUGARS	3G	6%
PROTEIN	32G	
VITAMIN D	0MCG	
CALCIUM	77MG	6%
IRON	3MG	15%
POTASSIUM	580MG	10%

CHAPTER 6

Sweets and Desserts

Low calorie desserts don't have to taste "light" … not at all! Nor do they have to take a lot of time to make. And with these recipes, there is absolutely no need to turn on a big oven to bake your desserts. The pressure cooker does the work and keeps the heat out of the kitchen!

Apple-Cranberry Oat Crumble

SERVES 4: ¾ CUP (193 G) PER SERVING

FOR TOPPING

½ cup (40 g) quick cooking or (78 g) old-fashioned rolled oats

1 ounce (28 g) chopped pecans

¼ teaspoon ground cinnamon

⅛ teaspoon ground nutmeg

1 tablespoon (15 g) packed dark brown sugar

¼ teaspoon salt

FOR BASE

1 cup plus 1 tablespoon (255 ml) water, divided

3 cups (375 g) chopped apples

2 tablespoons (15 g) dried cranberries, halved

1½ teaspoons cornstarch

2 tablespoons (30 g) packed dark brown sugar

1 tablespoon (14 g) light butter with canola oil

1 teaspoon vanilla extract

NOTE

Get the flavors and texture of home-baked without having to heat up the oven or kitchen or wait before you can actually eat it. Toasting the topping in the pressure cooker cooking pot first, then topping the cooked apple mixture with it are all that's needed.

Continued

To make the topping: On your pressure cooker, select Sauté/Browning + more to preheat the cooking pot. Once hot, add the oats, pecans, cinnamon, and nutmeg. Cook for 5 minutes, stirring frequently. Stir in the brown sugar and salt. Transfer the topping to a plate and set aside.

To make the base: In the pressure cooker cooking pot, combine 1 cup (240 ml) of water, the apples, and dried cranberries.

Lock the lid in place and close the seal valve. Press the Cancel button. Press the Manual button to set the cook time for 4 minutes. When the cook time ends, use a quick pressure release.

When the valve drops, carefully remove the lid. Press the Cancel button. Select Sauté/Browning + more. In a small bowl, whisk the remaining 1 tablespoon (15 ml) of water and the cornstarch until the cornstarch dissolves. Stir this slurry into the fruit mixture along with the brown sugar. Bring to a boil. Boil for 1 minute, stirring constantly. Turn off the pressure cooker. Stir in the butter and vanilla. Transfer the fruit mixture to a shallow bowl or casserole dish.

Top with the oat mixture and let stand 15 minutes to absorb the flavors.

NUTRITION FACTS

PER SERVING (193 G)

CALORIES	200	
		% DAILY VALUE
TOTAL FAT	7G	9%
SATURATED FAT	1G	5%
TRANS FAT	0G	
CHOLESTEROL	0MG	
SODIUM	60MG	3%
TOTAL CARBOHYDRATE	33G	12%
DIETARY FIBER	5G	18%
TOTAL SUGARS	20G	
ADDED SUGARS	6G	12%
PROTEIN	2G	
VITAMIN D	0MCG	
CALCIUM	17MG	2%
IRON	1MG	6%
POTASSIUM	175MG	4%

Upside-Down Chocolate-Crusted Cheesecake

SERVES 8: ⅛ CAKE AND 1 COOKIE PER SERVING

Nonstick cooking spray, for preparing the pan

12 ounces (340 g) light cream cheese, at room temperature

½ cup (115 g) 2% plain Greek yogurt

⅓ cup (67 g) sugar

1 tablespoon (8 g) all-purpose flour

1 teaspoon vanilla extract

3 large eggs, at room temperature

1 cup (240 ml) water

8 chocolate wafers, such as Nabisco Famous, crushed

1 cup (15 g) fresh raspberries (optional)

NOTE

Cheesecake with eggs, cream cheese, sugar, AND chocolate . . . really? By using reduced-fat cream cheese, a small amount of sugar, only 1 egg yolk, and crumbling a few chocolate cookies on top, you can have it all.

Continued

Coat an 8-inch (20 cm) springform pan with cooking spray and set aside.

In a blender, combine the cream cheese, yogurt, sugar, flour, vanilla, and 1 egg. Separate the remaining 2 eggs and add the egg whites to the blender. Discard the remaining yolks, or save for another use. Purée the ingredients until blended.

Place the water in the cooking pot and set a trivet in the pot. Pour the cheesecake batter into the prepared pan. Wrap the entire pan with aluminum foil. Make a foil sling by folding a 20-inch (50 cm)-long piece of foil in half lengthwise. Place the pan in the center of the sling and lower the pan into the pot. Fold down the excess foil from the sling to allow the lid to close properly. (Note: The pan will fit snuggly in the cooking pot.)

Lock the lid in place and close the seal valve. Press the Manual button to set the cook time for 23 minutes. When the cook time ends, use a natural release.

When the valve drops, carefully remove the lid. Let the cheesecake rest for 5 minutes in the cooking pot. Use the foil sling to remove the cheesecake from the pot and place it on a wire rack to cool for 1 hour. Cover and refrigerate overnight, or for at least 8 hours, before serving.

Release and remove the sides of pan. Cut the cheesecake into 8 wedges and sprinkle each with an equal amount of crushed cookies. Top with the fresh raspberries, if desired.

NUTRITION FACTS

PER SERVING (87 G)

CALORIES	170	
	% DAILY VALUE	
TOTAL FAT	8G	10%
SATURATED FAT	4.5G	23%
TRANS FAT	0G	
CHOLESTEROL	50MG	17%
SODIUM	230MG	10%
TOTAL CARBOHYDRATE	18G	7%
DIETARY FIBER	0G	
TOTAL SUGARS	14G	
ADDED SUGARS	8G	16%
PROTEIN	7G	
VITAMIN D	0MCG	
CALCIUM	81MG	6%
IRON	0MG	
POTASSIUM	145MG	4%

Banana Chocolate Chip Peanut Butter Wedges

SERVES 8: ⅛ CAKE AND 2 TABLESPOONS (18.75 G) BANANAS PER SERVING

Nonstick cooking spray, for preparing the pan

1 package (7.4-ounce, or 210 g) chocolate chip muffin mix

½ cup (120 ml) 2% milk

⅛ teaspoon ground nutmeg

1 cup (240 ml) water

2 tablespoons (32 g) natural peanut butter or almond butter

1 cup (150 g) chopped bananas

1½ teaspoons sugar

½ teaspoon ground cinnamon

NOTE

These thin cakelike wedges are topped with a layer of nut butter and served smothered with chopped bananas and cinnamon sugar. You'll feel like a kid again with every bite!

Coat an 8-inch (20 cm) spring form pan with cooking spray and set aside.

In a medium bowl, stir together the muffin mix, milk, and nutmeg just until blended. Do not overmix.

Place the water in the cooking pot and set a trivet in the pot. Pour the batter into the prepared pan. Wrap the entire pan with aluminum foil. Make a foil sling by folding a 20-inch (50 cm)-long piece of foil in half lengthwise. Place the pan in the center of the sling and lower the pan into the pot. Fold down the excess foil from the sling to allow the lid to close properly. (Note: The pan will fit snuggly in the cooking pot.)

Lock the lid in place and close the seal valve. Press the Manual button to set the cook time for 10 minutes. When the cook time ends, use a quick pressure release.

When the valve drops, carefully remove the lid. Use the sling to remove the pan from the cooking pot and place it on wire rack. Remove the foil.

Using the back of a spoon, spread the peanut butter evenly over the cake. Let cool completely. (Note: The texture will change while cooling.)

Release and remove the sides of the pan. Cut the cake into 8 wedges. Top with the bananas. In a small bowl, stir together the sugar and cinnamon and sprinkle evenly over all.

NUTRITION FACTS

PER SERVING (65 G)

CALORIES	170	
	% DAILY VALUE	
TOTAL FAT	6G	8%
SATURATED FAT	2.5G	13%
TRANS FAT	0G	
CHOLESTEROL	5MG	2%
SODIUM	140MG	6%
TOTAL CARBOHYDRATE	25G	9%
DIETARY FIBER	1G	4%
TOTAL SUGARS	14G	
ADDED SUGARS	1G	2%
PROTEIN	3G	
VITAMIN D	0MCG	
CALCIUM	94MG	8%
IRON	2MG	10%
POTASSIUM	88MG	2%

Lemon-Berry Bread Pudding

SERVES 4: 1 BREAD PUDDING, 2 TABLESPOONS (30 ML) SAUCE,
AND ¼ CUP (42.5 G) BERRIES PER SERVING

FOR BREAD PUDDING

Nonstick cooking spray, for preparing the ramekins

½ cup (120 ml) 2% milk

2 large eggs

1½ teaspoons vanilla extract

1½ teaspoons grated lemon zest

⅛ teaspoon ground cinnamon

4 ounces (115 g) French bread, cut into 1-inch (2.5 cm) cubes

1 cup (240 ml) water

FOR SAUCE

⅓ cup (80 ml) water

3 tablespoons (37.5 g) sugar

2 teaspoons cornstarch

1 teaspoon grated lemon zest

1 tablespoon (15 ml) fresh lemon juice

2 teaspoons light butter with canola oil

1 cup (170 g) quartered fresh strawberries or (145 g) blueberries

NOTE

You don't often think of a dessert as providing much in the way of protein, but this one is deliciously packed with 7 grams in every serving!

To make the bread pudding: In a medium bowl, whisk the milk, eggs, vanilla, lemon zest, and cinnamon. Add the bread cubes and toss gently until well coated.

Coat four 6-ounce (170 g) ramekins or custard cups with cooking spray. Equally divide the bread pudding among the prepared ramekins. Wrap each ramekin entirely with aluminum foil.

Place the water in the cooking pot and set a trivet in the pot. Place 3 ramekins on the trivet and place the remaining ramekin on top.

Lock the lid in place and close the seal valve. Press the Manual button to set the cook time for 20 minutes. When the cook time ends, use a natural pressure release for 10 minutes, then a quick pressure release.

When the valve drops, carefully remove the lid. Using rubber-tipped tongs or a think dish towel, remove the ramekins from the pot and place them on a wire rack. Remove the foil and let stand for 10 minutes to cool slightly.

To make the sauce: Meanwhile, in a small bowl, combine the water, sugar, cornstarch, lemon zest, and lemon juice. Stir until the cornstarch dissolves completely.

Remove the trivet from the pot and discard the water. Press the Cancel button. Select Sauté/Browning + more to preheat the cooking pot. Once hot, add the sauce. Bring to a boil. Boil for 1 minute, or until thickened, stirring constantly. Pour the sauce back into the small bowl. Stir in the butter and let cool slightly. Top the bread pudding with equal amounts of the sauce and berries.

NUTRITION FACTS

PER SERVING (140 G)

CALORIES 200

		% DAILY VALUE
TOTAL FAT	4.5G	6%
SATURATED FAT	1.5G	8%
TRANS FAT	0G	
CHOLESTEROL	95MG	32%
SODIUM	240MG	10%
TOTAL CARBOHYDRATE	30G	11%
DIETARY FIBER	1G	4%
TOTAL SUGARS	14G	
ADDED SUGARS	10G	20%
PROTEIN	7G	
VITAMIN D	1MCG	6%
CALCIUM	73MG	6%
IRON	2MG	10%
POTASSIUM	174MG	4%

Mini Flans with Espresso

SERVES 4: 1 FLAN AND 1½ TEASPOONS ESPRESSO PER SERVING

⅔ cup (160 ml) fat-free evaporated milk

½ cup (120 ml) 2% milk

⅓ cup (107 g) pure maple syrup

2 large eggs

1 teaspoon vanilla extract

⅛ teaspoon ground nutmeg

⅛ teaspoon salt

Nonstick cooking spray, for preparing the ramekins

1 cup (240 ml) water

FOR ESPRESSO

2 tablespoons (30 ml) water

1 teaspoon sugar

¼ teaspoon instant coffee granules

¼ teaspoon vanilla extract

In a medium bowl, whisk the evaporated milk, 2% milk, maple syrup, eggs, vanilla, nutmeg, and salt.

Coat four 6-ounce (180 ml) ramekins or custard cups with cooking spray. Place an equal amount of the egg mixture in each ramekin. Wrap each entirely with aluminum foil.

Put a trivet into the pressure cooker cooking pot and pour in the water. Place 3 ramekins on the trivet and top with the remaining ramekin.

Lock the lid in place and close the seal valve. Press the Manual button to set the cook time for 8 minutes. When the cook time ends, use a natural pressure release for 10 minutes, then a quick release.

When the valve drops, carefully remove the lid. Transfer the ramekins to a cooling rack. Carefully remove the foil. Cool completely. Cover and refrigerate until serving.

To make the espresso: In a cup or small bowl, stir together the espresso ingredients until the sugar dissolves.

When serving, invert the ramekins onto 4 dessert plates and spoon equal amounts of espresso over each.

NUTRITION FACTS

SERVING SIZE (127 G)		
CALORIES	160	
	% DAILY VALUE	
TOTAL FAT	3G	4%
SATURATED FAT	1G	5%
TRANS FAT	0G	
CHOLESTEROL	95MG	32%
SODIUM	170MG	7%
TOTAL CARBOHYDRATE	26G	9%
DIETARY FIBER	0G	
TOTAL SUGARS	24G	
ADDED SUGARS	17G	34%
PROTEIN	7G	
VITAMIN D	2MCG	10%
CALCIUM	201MG	15%
IRON	1MG	6%
POTASSIUM	277MG	6%

NOTE

Wrapping each custard dish entirely with aluminum foil prevents any water or steam from getting into the egg mixture. Use tongs or a clean cloth to remove each dish easily and safely when finished cooking.

Pumpkin Pot

SERVES 8: ABOUT ½ CUP (97 G) PER SERVING. COVER AND REFRIGERATE
ANY LEFTOVERS FOR UP TO 24 HOURS.

Nonstick cooking spray, for preparing the pan

½ cup (55 g) chopped pecans

8 ginger snap cookies, crushed

1 can (15 ounces, or 425 g) solid-pack pumpkin

½ cup (120 ml) fat-free sweetened condensed milk

1 large egg

2 tablespoons (30 g) packed brown sugar

½ teaspoon ground cinnamon

¼ teaspoon ground nutmeg

¼ teaspoon ground ginger

¼ teaspoon salt

½ teaspoon vanilla, butter, and nut flavoring or 1 teaspoon vanilla extract

1 cup (240 ml) water

NOTE

Made in a pan, but scooped like a pudding . . . this technique keeps things simple without using a lot of pans or dishes. You can find vanilla, butter, and nut flavoring next to the vanilla extract in your supermarket's spice aisle. It gives a butterscotch flavor to dishes.

Coat an 8-inch (20 cm) spring form pan with cooking spray and set aside.

On your pressure cooker, select Sauté/Browning + more to preheat the cooking pot. Once hot, add the pecans. Cook for 5 minutes, stirring frequently, until fragrant. Transfer the pecans to a cutting board and finely chop. Set aside in a small bowl and stir in the crushed ginger snaps. Turn off the pressure cooker.

In a medium bowl, combine the remaining ingredients except the water. Stir until well blended.

Place the water in the cooking pot and set a trivet in the pot. Pour the pumpkin mixture into the prepared pan. Wrap the entire pan with aluminum foil. Make a foil sling by folding a 20-inch (50 cm)-long piece of foil in half lengthwise. Place the pan in the center of the sling and lower the pan into the pot. Fold down the excess foil from the sling to allow the lid to close properly. (Note: The pan will fit snuggly in the cooking pot.)

Lock the lid in place and close the seal valve. Press the Manual button to set the cook time for 35 minutes. When the cook time ends, use a quick pressure release.

When the valve drops, carefully remove the lid. Use the foil sling to remove the pan and place it on a wire rack. Remove the foil and let stand for 1 hour. Refrigerate for 4 hours.

Spoon the chilled pumpkin mixture into individual dessert cups and top with equal amounts of the pecan mixture.

NUTRITION FACTS

PER SERVING (97 G)

CALORIES	170	
		% DAILY VALUE
TOTAL FAT	7G	9%
SATURATED FAT	1G	5%
TRANS FAT	0G	
CHOLESTEROL	25MG	8%
SODIUM	140MG	6%
TOTAL CARBOHYDRATE	26G	9%
DIETARY FIBER	2G	7%
TOTAL SUGARS	19G	
ADDED SUGARS	3G	6%
PROTEIN	4G	
VITAMIN D	0MCG	
CALCIUM	81MG	6%
IRON	2MG	10%
POTASSIUM	177MG	4%

Acknowledgments

To Dan Rosenberg, my editorial director, whose support and belief in me over the years has blossomed into a strong, forward-thinking relationship—it's fun working with you, Dan!

To Melanie McKibbin, my office manager, who swoops in, handles the office concerns and keeps me and the office in smooth running order. Thanks to your professionalism…and a smile—you add calm collectiveness to the daily chaos of it all! A good chaos, though!

To Sylvia Vollmer, my right hand in the kitchen. Thank goodness you provide eagerness and willingness to be by my side during the longest days that flow over into longer nights sometimes. You're always trying to figure out ways to contribute and conscientious enough to make sure things are "in order" at the end of your day so I can keep going and "function" after you clock out!

About the Author

Nancy S. Hughes writes for a wide range of health and food magazines and is the author of seventeen cookbooks, with a focus on low-calorie cooking for weight loss, heart-healthy cooking, diabetic cooking, and cooking with kitchen appliances. She lives in the Mobile, Alabama, area.

Index